# *THE TALMUD UNMASKED*

# *THE TALMUD UNMASKED*

## *THE SECRET RABBINICAL TEACHINGS CONCERNING CHRISTIANS*

*By*

***Rev. I. B. Pranaitis***
**(Roman Catholic Priest)**

***With Ecclesiastical Imprimatur***

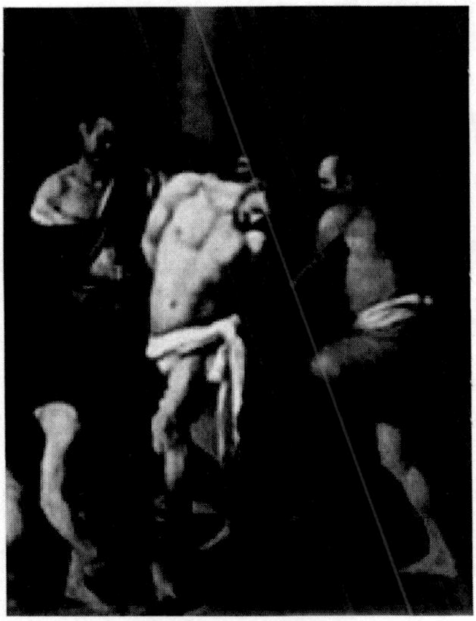

***"Forsaken by His own."***

KALPAZ

ISBN: 978-93-5128-573-1

First Published in 1892
Indian Reprint in 2017

*Published by*

Kalpaz Publications
C-30, Satyawati Nagar,
Delhi – 110052
E-mail: kalpaz@hotmail.com
Website: kalpazpublications.com
Ph.: +91-9212142040

**Cataloging in Publication Data—DK**
Courtesy: D.K. Agencies (P) Ltd. <docinfo@dkagencies.com>

**Pranai˜ti˜s, I. B. (IU!sti˜n Bonaventura), -1917, author.**
[Christianus in Talmude Iudaeorum. English]
The Talmud unmasked : the secret rabbinical teachings concerning Christians : with ecclesiastical imprimatur / by Rev. I.B. Pranaitis.
pages cm
Translated from Latin.
Translation of: Christianus in Talmude Iudaeorum.
"First published in 1892"—Title page verso.
ISBN 9789351285731

1. Judaism—Relations—Christianity. 2. Jesus Christ—Jewish interpretations. 3. Talmud. 4. Christianity and other religions—Judaism. I. Title.

BM509.C5P73 2017 DDC 296.1 23

# ANTIPHONE

“Let our writings be open to all people. Let them see what out moral code is like! We need not be afraid of this test, for we have a pure heart and a clean spirit. Let the nations investigate the habitations of the children of Israel, and of their own accord convince themselves of what they are really like! They will then exclaim for certain with Balaam, when he went out to curse Israel: *‘How beautiful are thy tents O Israel: how beautiful thy homes!’*

“In its attitude towards non-Jews, the Jewish religion is the most tolerant of the the religions in the world... The precepts of the ancient Rabbis, though inimical to Gentiles, cannot be applied in any way to Christians."

“A whole series of opinions can be quoted from the writings of the highest Rabbinical authorities to prove that these teachers inculcated in their own people a great love and respect for Christians, in order that they might look upon Christians, who believe in the true God, as brothers, and pray for them.”

“We hereby declare the the Talmud does not contain anything inimical to Christians.”

# PROLOGUE

Many people who are interested in the Jewish question are wont to ask whether or not there is anything in the Talmud which is not beautiful and sublime, and entirely removed from anything like hatred of Christians. The confusion of opinion about the matter is so great, that to listen to those who argue so wisely about it, you would think that they were discussing a very ancient and remote race of people, and not the people of Israel who live in our midst according to an unchanging moral code by which the religious and social life of the Jews has been regulated to this day.

This being so, I have undertaken to show what the Talmud really teaches about Christians, and thus satisfy the wishes of those who desire to find out about this doctrine from genuine original sources.

To this end I have translated the best known Talmudic books which refer to the Christians, and have arranged these sources in such order as to bring out clearly the picture of a Christian as represented to the Jews by the Talmud.

Lest I be accused of using a corrupted text of the Talmud or of not having interpreted it correctly, as is generally the case with those who have attempted to disclose secret Jewish teachings, I have placed the Hebrew text opposite the Latin.

I have divided the whole into two sections, the first of which treats of the teachings of the Talmud about Christians, and the other, the rules which Jews are obliged to follow when living among the Christians.

I preface these with a brief discussion about the Talmud itself in the following chapter.

# THE TALMUD

The Talmud gets its name from the word Lamud - *taught,* and means *The Teaching.* By metonymy it is taken to mean the book which contains the Teaching, which is called Talmud, that is, the doctrinal book which alone fully expounds and explains all the knowledge and teaching of the Jewish people.

As to the origin of the Talmud, the Rabbis regard Moses as its first author. They hold that, besides the written law which Moses received from God on Mount Sinai on tables of stone, which is called *Torah Schebiktab,* he also received interpretations of it, or the oral law, which is called *Torah Shebeal Peh.* They say that this is the reason why Moses remained so long on the mountain, as God could have given him the written law in one day.

Moses is said to have transmitted this oral law to Joshua; Joshua in turn to the seventy Elders; the Elders to the Prophets, and the Prophets to the Great Synagogue. It is held that it was later transmitted successively to certain Rabbis until it was no longer possible to retain it orally.

Whatever may be said about this story of the Rabbis, it is sufficiently known to us that before the birth of Christ, schools existed in Palestine in which sacred literature was taught. The commentaries of the Doctors of the law were noted down on charts and lists as an aid to memory, and these, when collected together, formed the beginnings of the Jewish Talmud.

In the second century after Christ, Rabbi Jehuda who, because of the sanctity of his life, was called The Saint, and The Prince, realizing that the learning of the Jews was diminishing, that their oral law was being lost, and that the Jewish people were being dispersed, was the first to consider ways and means of restoring and preserving their oral law. He collected all the lists and charts and from them he made a book which was called the Sepher Mischnaioth, or *Mischnah* - a *Deuterosis,* or secondary law. He divided it into six parts, each of which was divided into many chapters. We shall consider these later.

The *Mischnah* is the foundation and the principal part of the whole Talmud. This book was accepted by the Jews everywhere and was recognized as their authentic code of law. It was expounded in their Academies in Babylon - at

Sura, Iumbaditha and Nehardea - and in their Academies in Palestine - at Tiberias, Iamnia and Lydda.

As their interpretations increased with the passing of time, the disputations and decisions of the doctors of the law concerning the *Mischnah* were written down, and these writings constituted another part of the Talmud called the *Gemarah.*

These two parts are so disposed throughout the whole Talmud that the *Mischnah* serves first as a kind of text of the law, and is followed by the *Gemarah* as an analysis of its various opinions leading to definite decisions.

All the precepts of the *Mischnah,* however, were not discussed in the Jewish schools. Those whose use was nullified by the destruction of the Temple, and those whose observation was possible only in the Holy Land were not commented upon. Their explanation was left until the coming of Elias and the Messiah. For this reason some parts of the *Mischnah* are lacking in the *Gemarah.*

In interpreting the *Mischnah* of Rabbi Jehuda, the schools of Palestine and Babylon followed each their own method, and by thus following their own way gave rise to a twofold *Gemarah* - the Jerusalem and the Babylonian versions. The author of the Jerusalem version was Rabbi Jochanan, who was head of the synagogue in Jerusalem for eighty years. He wrote thirty-nine chapters of commentaries on the *Mischnah* which he compiled in the year 230 A.D.

The Babylonian *Gemarah,* however, was not compiled by any one person, nor at any one time. Rabbi Aschi began it in 327 A.D and labored over it for sixty years. He was followed by Rabbi Maremar about the year 427 A.D., and it was completed by Rabbi Abina about the year 500 A.D. The Babylonian *Gemarah* has thirty-six chapters of interpretations.

This twofold *Gemarah,* added to the *Mischnah,* makes also a twofold Talmud: The Jerusalem version, which, on account of its brevity and obscurity, is not much used; and the Babylonian version, which has been held in the highest esteem by Jews of all times.

The *Gemarah* is followed by additions called *Tosephoth.* It was thus that Rabbi Chaia first styled his opinions on the *Mischnah* which were made by the doctors outside the schools were called *Baraietoth,* or extraneous opinions.

These Commentaries were further supplemented by other decisions called *Piske Tosephoth,* short theses and simple principles.

For nearly five hundred years after the Babylonian Talmud was completed, the study of literature was greatly hampered partly due to public calamities and partly owing to dissensions among the scholars. But in the eleventh century others wrote further additions to the Talmud. Chief among these were the *Tosephoth* of Rabbi Ascher.

Besides these there appeared the *Perusch* of Rabbi Moische ben Maimon, called by the Jews Rambam for short, by the Christians Maimonides, and by Rabbi Schelomo, Iarchi or Raschi.

Thus, the *Mischna, Gemarah, Tosephoth,* the marginal notes of Rabbi Ascher, the *Piske Tosephoth* and the *Perusch Hamischnaioth* of Maimonides, all collected into one, constitute a vast work which is called the Talmud.

* * * * *

The main parts of the Talmud, which we mentioned above, are six:

I. ZERAIM: concerning seeds. It treats of seeds, fruits, herbs, trees; of the ublic and domestic use of fruits, of different seeds, etc.

II. MOED: concerning festivals. It treats of the time when the Sabbath and other festivals are to begin, ended and celebrated.

III. NASCHIM: concerning women. It treats of marrying and repudiating ves, their duties, relations, sicknesses, etc.

IV. NEZIKIN: concerning damages. It treats of damages suffered by men and animals, penalties and compensations.

V. KODASCHIM: concerning holiness. It treats of sacrifices and various sacred rites.

VI. OHOROTH: concerning purifications. It treats of the soiling and urifying of vessels, bedclothes and other things.

Each of these six parts, which the Jews call *Schishah Sedarim* - six orders or ordinances - is divided into books or tracts, called *Massiktoth,* and the books into chapters, or*Perakim*.

I. ZERAIM. Contains eleven books or *Masechtoth.*

1. BERAKTOTH - Benedictions and prayers. Treats of liturgical les.
2 PEAH - Corner of a field. Treats of the corners and gleanings of hef ield...The olives and grapes to be left to the poor.
3. DEMAI - Doubtful things. Whether or not tithes must be paid on such.
4 KILAIM - Mixtures. Treats of various mixings of seeds.
5. SCHEBIITH - the Sevents. Treats of the Sabbatical Year.
6. TERUMOTH -Offerings and Oblations. The Heave offerings for the ests.
7. MAASEROTH - the Tithes, to be given to the Levites.
8. MAASER SCHENI - the Second Tithe.
9. CHALLAH - the Dough, the portion to be given thereof to the Priests.

10. ORLAH - the Uncircumcised. Treats about the fruits of a tree during the first three years after its plantings.
11. BIKKURIM - the First Fruits to be brought to the Temple.

II. MOED. Contains twelve Books or *Masechtoth.*

1. SCHABBATH - the Sabbath. Treats of kinds of work prohibited on hat day.
2. ERUBHIN - Combinations. Contains precepts about food for the Sabbath eve.
3. SCHEKALIM - Passover. Treats of the laws relating to the Feast of Passover and the Paschal Lamb.
4. SCHEKALIM - Shekel. Treats of the size and weight of the shekel.
5. IOMA - the Day of Atonement. Treats of prescriptions for that Day.
6. SUKKAH - the Tabernacle. Treats of the laws concerning the feast of Tabernacles.
7. BETSAH - the Egg of the Day of Feast. Treats of the kind of work prohibited and permitted on the festivals.
8. ROSCH HASCHANAH - New Year. Treats of the Feast of New Year.
9. TAANITH - Fasts. Treats of public fasts.
10. MEGILLAH - the Scroll. Treats of the reading of the Book of Esther. Contains the description of the Feast of Purim.
11. MOED KATON - Minor Feast. treats of laws relating to the days intervening between the first and last days of Pesach and Succoth.
12. CHAGIGAH - Comparison of rites on on the three feats of Pesach, Sukkoth and Tabernacles.

III. NASCHIM. Contains seven Books or *Masechtoth*

1. JEBBAMOTH - Sisters in Law. Treats of Levirate marriage.
2. KETHUBOTH - Marriage Deeds. Treats of dower and marriage settlements

.3 KIDDUSCHIN- Betrothals.

4. GITTIN - booklet on Divorces.
5. NEDARIM - Vows. Treats of vows and their annulment.
6. NAZIR - the Nazarite. Treats of the laws concerning the Nazarites and those who separate themselves from the world and consecrate themselves to God.
7. SOTAH - the Woman suspected of adultery.

IV. NEZIKIN. Contains ten Books or *Masechtoth.*

1. BABA KAMA - First Gate. Treats of Damages and Injuries and their remedies.
2. BABA METSIA - Middle Gate. Treats of laws concerning found property, concerning trust, concerning buying and selling, ending, hiring and renting.
3. BABA BATHRA - Last Gate. Treats of laws concerning real estate and commerce, mostly based on the traditional law. Also concerning ereditary succession.
4. SANHEDRIN - Courts. Treats of the courts and their proceedings, and the punishment of capital crimes.
5. MAKKOTH - Stripes. The 40 stripes (minus one) inflicted on iminals.
6. SCHEBUOTH - Oaths. Treats different kinds of oaths.
7. EDAIOTH - Testimonies. Contains a collection of traditional laws and decisions gathers from the testimonies of the distinguished teachers.
8. HORAIOTH- Decisions. Treats of the sentences of Judges and the punishment of transgressors.
9. ABHODAH ZARAH - Idolatry.
10. ABHOTH - Fathers. Treats of laws of the fathers. It is called also PIRKE ABHOTH.

V. KODASCHIM. Contains eleven Books or *Masechtoth.*

1. ZEBBACHIM -Sacrifices. Treats of animal sacrifices and the mode of their offering.
2. CHULIN - Profane things. Treats of the traditional manner of slaughtering animals for ordinary use.
3. MENACHOTH - Meat-offerings. Treats of meat-and-drink offerings.
4. BEKHOROTH - the First Born. Treats of the laws concerning the first born of man and animals.
5. ERAKHIN - Estimations. Treats of the mode in which persons dedicated to the Lord by a vow are legally appraised in order to be redeemed.
6. TEMURAH - Exchange. Treats of the laws concerning sanctified things having been exchanged.
7. MEILAH - Trespass, Sacrilege. Treats of the sins subject to the punishment of excision, and their expiation by sacrifices.
8. KERITHUTH - Excisions -Treats of the sins subject to thep unishment

of excision, and their expiation by sacrifices.

9. TAMID - the Daily Sacrifice- Describes the Temple services connected with the daily morning and evening offerings.

10. MIDDOTH - Measurements. Describes the measurements and description of the Temple.

11. KINNIM - the Birds' Nests. Treats of the sacrifices consisting of wls, the offerings of the poor, etc.

VI. TOHOROTH. Contains twelve Books or *Masechtoth.*

1. KELLIM - Vessels. Treats of the conditions under which domestic utensils, garments, etc. receive ritual cleanness.

2. OHOLOTH - Tents. Treats of tents and houses, and how polluted and purified.

3. NEGAIM - Plagues. Treats of the laws relating to Leprosy.

4. PARAH - the Heifer. Treats of the laws concerning the red heifer and the use of its ashes for the purification of the unclean.

5. TOHOROTH - Purifications. Treats of some lesser degrees of ncleanness lasting only until sunset.

6. MIKVAOTH - Wells. Treats of the conditions under which wells and reservoirs are fit to be used for ritual purifications.

7. NIDDAH - Menstruation. Treats of the legal uncleanness arising from certain conditions in women.

8. MAKSCHIRIN - Preparations. Treats of liquids that prepare and dispose seeds and fruits to receive ritual uncleanness.

9. ZABHIM - Concerning nightly pollution and gonorrhea. Treats on the uncleanness arising from such secretions.

10 TEBHUL IOM - Daily washing.

11. IADAIM - Hands. Treats of the ritual uncleanness of hands, according to the traditional law, and of their purification.

12. OKETSIN - Stalks of fruit. Treats of stalks and shells of fruit as conveying ritual uncleanness.

The complete Talmud contains 63 books in 524 chapters.

Added to these are four other shorts tracts, which have not been included in he regular Talmud. They have been added by later writers and xponents.

These four are:

MASSEKHETH SOPHERIM - the Tract of Scribes. Treats of the mode of writing the books of the law. Has 21 chapters.

EBHEL RABBETI - a large treatise on Mourning. Has 14 chapters. KALLAH - the Bride. On the acquisition of the bride. Has one chapter. MASSEKHETH DEREKH ERETS - the Conduct of Lide. Divided into RABBAH - major parts, and ZUTA - the minor parts. Has 16 chapters. At the end is added a special chapter - PEREK SCHALOM - on Peace.

* * *

Since the Talmud was such a voluminous and disordered work, there was a need of a compendium which would facilitate its study. To supply this need, therefore, Rabbi Isaac ben Jacob Alphassi, in 1032, published a Shorter Talmud, which he called *Halakhoth* - Constitutions. He omitted all lengthy discussions and preserved only those parts which had to do with the practical things of life. Since this work, however, had no order to it, it was not considered of great worth.

The first to issue a well ordered work on Jewish Law was Maimonides, styled the "Eagle of the Synagogue." In 1180 he produced his celebrated work *Miscnhah Torah* - Repetition of the Law, also called *Iad Chazakah* - the Strong Hand. It contains four parts or volumes and 14 books and includes the whole Talmud. Maimonides also included much philosophical discussion in this work and attempted to establish many laws of his own. Because of this he was excommunicated by his people and condemned to death. He fled to Egypt where he died in the year 1205.

In spite of this, the value of his work increased in time, and for a while an expurgated version was held in the highest esteem by the Jews. A drawback to this work is that it contains many laws which were of no value after the destruction of the Temple.

An edition of the work of Maimonides, expurgated of all his philosophical innovations and of all the old, useless laws, was edited in 1340, in strict accord with the ideas of the Rabbis, by Jacob ben Ascher, to which he gave the name *Arbaa Turim* - The Four Orders, which are:

I. ORACH CHAIIM: The seeds of Life, and treats of the daily life in the home and in the Synagogue.

II. IORE DEAH: which teaches knowledge about foods, purifications and other religious laws.

III. CHOSCHEN HAMMISCHPAT: private judgments about civil and riminal laws.

IV. EBHEN HAEZER: The Rock of Help, which treats of the laws of marriage.

Since Alphasi, Maimonides and Jacob ben Ascher disagreed on many points, which gave rise to different interpretations of the same law, there was great need of a book which would contain short, concise solutions to controversies, and which would supply to the Jewish people a law book worthy of; the name.

Joseph Karo, a Rabbi of Palestine (born 1488, died 1577), supplied this need by his celebrated; commentary on the *Arbaa Turim,* which he called *Schulchan Arukh* - the Prepared Table. Since, however, the customs of oriental Jews differed greatly from those of western Jews, even the *Schulchan Arukh,* of Joseph Karo did not suffice for Jews everywhere. And for this reason Rabbi Mosche Isserles wrote a commentary on the *Schulchan Arukh,* entitled *Darkhe Mosche,* the Way of Moses, which received the same acceptance in the West as the work of Joseph Karo in the East.

At the present time, the *Schulchan Arukh* is regarded as the obligatory Law Code of the Jews, and they use it principally in their studies. Many commentaries have been written on each part of this book.

An important point to note is that this work has always been regarded by the Jews as holy. They have always held it, and still hold it, as more important than the Sacred Scriptures. The Talmud itself shows this very clearly:

Likewise in the tract *Sopherim* XV, 7, fol. 13b:

"The Sacred Scriptures is like water, the *Mischnah* wine, and the *Gemarah* aromatic wine.

The following is a well-known and highly praised opinion in the ritings of the Rabbis:

"My son, give heed to the words of the scribes rather than to the words of

Vthe law."

The reason for this is found in the tract *Sanhedrin* X, 3, f.88b:

"He who transgresses the words of the scribes sins more gravely than the transgressors of the words of the law."

Also when there are differences of opinion between the Law and the doctors, both must be taken as the words of the Lord God.

In the tract *Erubhin*, f.13b, where it is related that there was a difference of opinion between the two schools of Hillel and Schamai, it is concluded that:

"The words of both are the words of the living God."

In the book *Mizbeach*, cap. V, we find the following opinion:

"There is nothing superior to the Holy Talmud."

Contemporary defenders of the Talmud speak of it almost in the same way.

What Christians have thought of the Talmud is amply proved by the many edicts and decrees issued about it, by which the supreme rulers in Church and State proscribed it many times and condemned this sacred Secondary Law Code of the Jews to the flames.

In 553 the Emperor Justinian forbade the spread of the Talmudic books throughout the Roman Empire. In the 13th century "Popes Gregory IX and Innocent IV condemned the books of the Talmud as containing every kind of vileness and blasphemy against Christian truth, and ordered them to be burned because they spread many horrible heresies."

Later, they were condemned by many other Roman Pontiffs - Julius III, Paul IV, Pius IV, Pius V, Gregory XIII, Clement VIII, Alexander VII, Benedict XIV, and by others who issued new editions of the Index of Forbidden Books according to the orders of the Fathers of the Council of Trent, and even in our own time.

At the beginning of the 16th century, when the peace of the Church was disturbed by new religions, the Jews began to distribute the Talmud openly, aided by the art of printing then recently invented. The first printed edition of the whole Talmud, containing all its blasphemies against the Christian religion, was published in Venice in the year 1520. And almost all Jewish books published in that century, which was favorable to them, are complete and genuine.

Towards the end of the 16th century and at the beginning of the 17th, when many famous men undertook diligently to study the Talmud, the Jews, fearing for themselves, began to expunge parts of the Talmud which was published at Basle in 1578 has been mutilated in many places.

And at Synod in Poland, in the year 1631, the Rabbis of Germany and many other countries declared that nothing which would annoy the Christians and cause persecution of Israel, should be printed. For this reason there are signs of many things missing in the Jewish books which were published in the following century and thereafter. The Rabbis explain from memory what these things mean, for they possess the genuine books which Christians rarely see.

However, Jewish books were published later with very few mutilations in Holland - where the Jews who were expelled from Spain were kindly received. The Talmud published there in 1644 - 1648 is almost similar to the Venetian edition.

The latest device invented to deceive the censors was to insert the word *haiah* (was) with the genuine text, as if to indicate that the matter in question once had its place there. But by so doing they only cleanse the outside of the cup. For in many places they do show what they mean, ex.gr. by the words *gam attah*, "even now," *viz.* "this law obliges"; and *aphilu bazzeman hazzeh,* "even to this day" *viz.* "this law holds," and such like.

We must add a few remarks about that other very well known book of the

Jews, called the ZOHAR.

According to some Rabbis, Moses, after he had been instructed in the interpretation of the law on Mount Sinai, did not pass this information to Joshua nor he to the Elders, but to Aaron, Aaron to Eleazer, and so on until the oral teachings had been put into book form called the ZOHAR, so called from the name ZEHAR, meaning to shine forth. For it is an illustration of the books of Moses, a commentary on the Pentateuch.

The author is said to have been R. Schimeon ben Jochai, a disciple of R. Akibha who, fifty years after the destruction of the Temple, ended his life as a martyr about the year 120 A.D. in Hadrian's war against the Jews. Since, however, names of men appear in this book who lived many centuries after the year indicated, and since neither Rambam (R. Mosche ben Nachman), nor R. Ascher, who died about the year 1248 A.D., make no mention of it, it is more likely that those are nearer the truth who say that the book of Zohar first saw the light about the 13th century. Especially is this considered likely since about this time a book was produced which is similar in argument and style to the Chaldaic type of writing.

It consists of three volumes in large octavo.

Many other works have been published by the Jewish teachers which are used in the study of Jewish law, and which are held in high esteem since they explain many obscure passages in the Talmud. Some of them are cited in this book, and are as follows:

BIAR - Declaration, elucidation, Commentary on another Commentary. These declarations differ from one another.

HALAKOTH - usually written HILKHOTH - Decisions or Dissertations. Separate books of Holy Scriptures and of the Talmud by different Rabbis: Maimonides, Beshai, Edels, Moses of Kotzen, Kimchi and others. In most cases citations are given from HILKOTH AKUM by Maimonides. These contain dissertations on stars and planets and the status of nations. There is another - HILKOTH MAAKHALOTH ASAVOROTH - dissertation about forbidden foods.

IUCHASIN or SEPHER IUCHASIN - dissertations on lineage. Treats of Sacred and Jewish history from the beginning of the world until 1500. Printed at Cracow, 1580.

JALKUT - a collected commentary from various ancient books. Supposed to have not a literal but allegorical meaning. Author: Rabbi Shimeon of Frankfurt.

KED HAKKEMACH - Barrel of flour. Contains places of theological communities in alphabetical order. Author: Rabbi Bechai of Lublin.

MAGEN ABRAHAM - Shield of Abraham. Author: Perizola.

MIZBEACH HAZZAHABH - the Golden Altar. A Cabalistic book. Author: R. Schelomon ben Rabbi Mordechai. Printed at Basle, in 1602.

MACHZOR - a Cycle. Book of Prayers used on great festivals.

MENORATH HAMMAOR - Candlestick of light. A Talmudic book. Contains Aggadoth and Medraschim. i.e., allegorical and historical comments on the entire Talmud. Author: Rabbi Isaac Abhuhabh. Printed in 1544.

MAIENE HAIESCHUAH - Fountains of the Savior. An exquisite Commentary on Daniel by Rabbi Isaac Abarbanel. There are numerous disputations against Christians. Printed in 1551.

MIKRA GEDOLAH - the Great Convocation. A Hebrew Bible with commentaries by R. Salomon Iarchi and R. Ezra.

MASCHMIA IESCHUAH - The Preacher of Salvation. Explanations on all the Prophets. On future redemption. Author: R. Abarbanel.

NIZZACHON - Victory. Attacks on Christians and on the Four Gospels. Author: Rabbi Lipman. Printed in 1559.

SEPHER IKKARIM - Book on fundamentals or articles of faith. It contains one very bitter attack against the Christian faith.

EN ISRAEL - the Eye of Israel. A celebrated book. Has a second part - BETH JAKOBH - the House of Jacob. Embraces the most delightful Talmudic histories. Printed in Venice, in 1547.

SCHAARE ORAH - the Gates of Light. A most celebrated Cabalistic book. Author: Ben Joseph Gekatilia.

SCHEPHAA TAL - Abundance of Dew. A Cabalistic book. A key to the book of Zohar and other similar books. Author: Rabbi Schephtel Horwitz of Prague.

TOLDOTH IESCHU - the Generations of Jesus. A little pamphlet full of blasphemies and maledictions. Contains the history of Christ. Full of false and deceiving manifestations.

In preparing this booklet I have used the following source material:

The TALMUD. Edition of Amsterdam, 1644-48, in 14 volumes.

SCHULKHAN ARUKH, by Rabbi Joseph Karo. Edition of Venice, 1594. Without commentaries.

IORE DEAH. Numerous quotations. Edition of Krakow.

ZOHAR. Edition of Amsterdam, 1805. 3 volumes.

MIKRA GEDOLAH. Edition of Amsterdam, 1792, 12 volumes, edition of Basle, 1620, 2 volumes, edition of Venice.

HILKHOTH AKUM, of R. Maimonides, edition by Vossius, 1675

As auxillary works I have used:

JOANNES BUXDORFIUS. a Lexicon Chaldaicum, Talmudicum et Rabbinicum, Base, 1640. b. De Abreviaturis Hebraicis; Operis Talmudis Recensio; Biblicothea Rabbinica. Basle, 1712. c. Synagoga Judaica. Basle, 1712.

JOH. CHRISTOPHORI WAGENSEILII, Sota. Aldtorfi Noricum, 1674.

GEORGII ELIEZ EDZARDI: Tractatus talmudici "AVODA SARA." Hamburg, 1705.

JACOBI ECKER: "Der Judenspiegel im Lichte der Wahrheit," (The Jewish Mirror in the Light of Truth). Paderborn, 1884.

AUGUST ROHLING: Die Polemik und das Manschenopfer des Rabbinismus. (The Polemics and Human Sacrifice of Rabbinism). Paderborn, 1883.

I have only used the works of those who are held in the highest esteem by the Jews themselves, and to whom the Jews appeal when disputing with Christians, by quoting impartially the opinions of these learned men. Their great dilligence in quoting from the texts of books which I was able to examine, has been a proof to me that I used the same diligence even in quoting from less known sources to which they have much greater access than I.

# PART ONE

# THE TEACHING OF THE TALMUD CONCERNING CHRISTIANS

First we shall see what the Talmud teaches about Jesus Christ, the founder of Christianity; and secondly, about his followers, the Christians.

# CHAPTER I

# JESUS CHRIST IN THE TALMUD

Many passages in the Talmudic books treat of the birth, life, death, and teachings of Jesus Christ. He is not always referred to by the same name, however, but is diversely called " That Man," "A Certain One," "The Carpenter's Son," "The One Who Was Hanged," etc.

**Article I. - Concerning the Names of Jesus Christ**

1. The real name of Christ in Hebr ew is *Jeschua Hanotsri* - Jesus the Nazarene. He is called *Notsri* from the city of Nazareth in which he was brought up. Thus in the Talmud Christians also are called *Notsrim* - Nazarenes.
Since the word *Jeschua* means "Savior," the name Jesus rarely occurs in the Jewish books. It is almost always abbreviated to *Jeschu,* which is maliciously taken as if it were composed of the initial letters of the three words Immach Schemo Vezikro - "May his name and memory be blotted out."

2. In the Talmud Christ is called *Otho Isch* - "That man," i.e. the one who is known to all. In the tract *Abhodah Zarah,* 6a, we read: "He is called a Christian who follows the false teachings of *that man,* who taught them to celebrate the feast on the first day of the Sabbath, that is, to worship on the first day after the Sabbath"

3. Elsewhere he is simply called *Peloni* - "A Certain One." In *hagigah,* 4b, we read: "Mary...the mother of a certain one, of whom it is related in *Schabbath..."* (104b) That this Mary is none other than the mother of Jesus will be shown later.

4. Out of contempt, Jesus is also called *Naggar bar naggar* - "the carpenter son of a carpenter", also *Ben charsch etaim* - "the son of a wood worker."

5. He is also called *Talui* - "The one who was hanged." Rabbi Samuel, the son of Mair, in the *Hilch. Akum* of Maimonides, refers to the fact that it was

forbidden to take part in the Christian feats of Christmas and Easter because they were celebrated *on account of him who was hanged.* And Rabbi Aben Ezra, in a commentary on *Genes.* also calls him *Talui,* whose image the Emperor Constantine reproduced on his banner. "...in the days of Constantine, who made a change of religion and placed the figure of *the one who was hanged* on his banner."

**Article II. - The Life of Christ**

The Talmud teaches that Jesus Christ was illegitimate and was conceived during menstruation; that he had the soul of Esau; that he was a fool, a conjurer, a seducer; that he was crucified, buried in hell and set up as an idol ever since by his followers.

1. ILLEGITIMATE AND CONCEIVED DURING MENSTRUATION The following is narrated in the Tract *Kallah,* 1b:

"Once when the Elders were seated at the Gate, two young men passed by, one of whom had his covered, the other with his head bare. Rabbi Eliezer remarked that the one in his bare head was illegitimate, a *mamzer.* Rabbi Jehoschua said that he was conceived during menstruation, *ben niddah.* Rabbi Akibah, however, said that he was both. Whereupon the others asked Rabbi Akibah why he dared to contradict his colleagues. He answered that he could prove what he said. He went therefore to the boy's mother whom he saw sitting in the market place selling vegetables and said to her: "My daughter, if you will answer truthfully what I am going to ask you, I promise that you will be saved in the next life." She demanded that he would swear to keep his promise, and Rabbi Akibah did so - but with his lips only, for in his heart he invalidated his oath. Then he said: "Tell me, what kind of son is this of yours"? To which she replied: "The day I was married I was having menstruation, and because of this my husband left me. But an evil spirit came and slept with me and from this intercourse my son was born to me." Thus it was proved that this young man was not only illegitimate but also conceived during the menstruation of his mother. And when his questioners heard this they declared: "Great indeed was Rabbi Akibah when he corrected his Elders"! And they exclaimed: "Blessed be the Lord God of Israel who revealed his secret to Rabbi Akibah the son of Joseph"!

That the Jews understand this story to refer to Jesus and his mother, Mary, is clearly demonstrated in their book *Toldath Jeschu* - "The Generations of Jesus" - where the birth of our Savior is narrated in almost the same words.

Another story of this kind is narrated in *Sanhedrin,* 67a: "Of all who are guilty of death by the Law, he alone is caught by a ruse. How is it done? They light a candle in an inner room and place witnesses in an adjoining room outside where they can see him and hear his voice, but where they cannot be seen by him. Then the one whom he tried to seduce says to him "Please repeat here privately what you told me before." If the seducer repeats what he said, the others ask him " But how shall we leave our God who is in heaven and serve idols?" If the seducer repents, then all is well.But if he says "This is our duty and it is right for us to do so," then the witnesses outside, who have heard him, bring him before the judge and stone him to death. This is what they did to the son of Stadi in Lud, and they hanged him on the eve of the Passover. Forthis son of Stada was the son of Pandira. For Rabbi Chasda tells us that Pandira was the husband of Stada, his mother, and he lived during the time Paphus the son of Jehuda. But his mother was stada, Mary of Magdala (a ladies' hairdresser) who, as it is said in Pumbadita, deserted her husband."

The meaning of this is that his Mary was called Stada, that is, a prostitute, because, according to what was taught at Pumbadita, she left her husband and commited adultery. This is also recorded in the Jerusalem Talmud and by Maimonides. That the mention here is of Mary, the mother of Jesus, is verified in the Tract *Chagigah,* 4b:

"When Rabbi Bibhai was visited once by the Death Angel (the devil), the latter said to his assistant: "Go and bring to me Mary the hairdresser" (that is, kill her). He went and brought Mary the children's hairdresser - in place of the other Mary."

A marginal note explains this passage as follows:

"This story of Mary the Ladies' hairdresser happened under the Second Temple. She was the mother of *Peloni,* "that man," as he is called in the tract *Schabbath."*

In *Schabbath* the passage referred to says:

"Rabbi Elizer said to the Elders: "Did not the son Stada practice Egyptian magic by cutting it into his flesh?" They replied: "He was a fool, and we do not pay attention to what fools do. The son of Stada, Pandra's son, etc." as above in *Sanhedrin,*67a.

This magic of the son of Stada is explained as follows in the book *Beth Jacobh,* fol. 127 a:

"The Magi, before they left Egypt, took special care not to put their agic in writing lest other peoples might come to learn it But he devised a new way by which he inscribed it on his skin, or made cuts in his skin and inserted it there and which, when the wounds healed up, did not show what they meant." Buxtorf says:

"There is little doubt who this Ben Stada was, or who the Jews understood him to be. Although the Rabbis in their additions to the Talmud try to hide their malice and say that it is not Jesus Christ, their deceit is plainly evident, and many things prove that they wrote and understood all these things about him. In the first place, they also call him the son of Pandira. Jesus the Nazarene is thus called in other passages of the Talmud where express mention is made of *Jesus the son of Pandira.* St. John Damascene also, in his Genealogy of Christ, mentions Panthera and the Son of Panthera.

"Secondly, this Stada is said to be Mary, and this Mary the mother of *Peloni* "that certain one," by which without doubt Jesus is meant. For in this way they were accustomed to cover up his name because they were afraid to mention it. If we had copies of the original manuscripts they would certainly prove this. And this also was the name of the mother of Jesus the Nazarene. "Thirdly, he is called the Seducer of the People. The Gospels testify that Jesus was called this by the Jews, and their writings to this day are proof that they still call him by this name.

"Fourthly, he is called "the one who was hanged," which clearly refers to the crucifixion of Christ, especially since a reference to the time "on the eve of the Passover" is added, which coincides with the time of the crucifixion of Jesus. In *Sanhedrin* they wrote as follows: "On the eve of the Passover they hanged Jesus"

"Fifthly, as to what the Jerusalem Talmud says about the two disciples of the Elders who were sent as witnesses to spy on him, and who were afterwards brought forward as witnesses against him: This refers to the two "false witnesses" of whom the Evangelists Matthew and Luke make mention.

"Sixthly, concerning what they say about the son of Stada that he practiced Egyptian magical arts by cutting into his flesh: the same accusation is made against Christ in their hostile book *Toldoth Jeschu.*

"Lastly, the time corresponds. For it is said that this son of Stada lived in the days of Paphus the son of Jehuda, who was a contemporary of Rabbi Akibah. Akibah, however, lived at the time of the Ascension of Christ, and for some time after. Mary is also said to have lived under the Second Temple. All this clearly proves that they secretly and blasphemously understand this son of Stada to be Jesus Christ the son of Mary.

"Other circumstances may seem to contradict this. But that is nothing new in Jewish writings and is done on purpose so that Christians may detect their trickery."

2. Furthermore, "In the secret books, which are not permitted to falleasily into the hands of Christians, they say that the soul of Esau cameinto Christ, that he was therefore evil and that he was Esau himself."

3. By some he is called a FOOL and INSANE

In *Schabbath,* 104b:

"They, [the Elders] said to him [Eliezer]: "He was a fool, and no one pays attention to fools."

4. A CONJURER AND MAGICIAN

In the infamous book *Toldoth Jeschu,* our Savior is blasphemed as follows: "And Jesus said: Did not Isaiah and David, my ancestors, prophesy about me? *The Lord said to me, thou art my son, today I have begotten thee, etc.* Likewise in another place: *The Lord said to my Lord, sit thou at my right hand.* Now I ascend to my father who is in heaven and will sit at his right hand, which you will see with your own eyes.

But you, Judas, will never reach that high. Then Jesus pronounced the great name of God (IHVH) and continued to do so until a wind came and took him up between earth and sky. Judas also pronounced the name of God and he likewise was taken up by the wind. In this way they both floated around in the air to the amazement of the onlookers.

Then Judas, again pronouncing the Divine Nane, took hold of Jesus and pushed him down to earth. But Jesus tried to do the same to Judas and thus they fought together.

And when Judas saw he could not win out over the works of Jesushe pissed on Jesus, and both thus being unclean they fell to earth; nor could theyn use the Divine name again until they had washed themselves."

Whether those who believe such devilish lies deserve greater hatred or pity, I cannot say.

In another place in the same book it is related that in the house of the Sanctuary there was a stone which the Patriarch Jacob anointed with oil. On this stone were carved the tetragrammatic letters of the Name (IHVH), and if anyone could learn from them he could destroy the world. They therefore decreed that no one must learn them, and they placed two dogs upon two iron columns before the Sanctuary so that if anyone should learn them the dogs would bark at him coming out and he would forget the letters through fear. Then it is related: "Jesus came and entered, learned the letters and wrote them down on parchment. Then he cut into the flesh of his thigh and inserted them there, and having pronounced the name, the wound healed."

5. IDOLATER

In the Tract *Sanhedrin* (103a) the words of *Psalm* XCI, 10: "No plague shall come near thy dwelling," are explained as follows:

"That thou mayest never have a son or a disciple who will salt his food so much that he destroys his taste in public, like Jesus the Nazarene." To salt one's food too much or to destroy one's taste, is proverbially said of one who corrupts his morals or dishonors himself, or who falls into heresy and idolatry and openly preaches it to others.

6. SEDUCER:

In the same book *Sanhedrin* (107b) we read

"Mar said: Jesus seduced, corrupted and destroyed Israel."

7. CRUCIFIED

Finally as punishment for his crimes and impiety, he suffered an ignominious death by being hanged on a cross on the eve of the Passover (as we have seen above).

8. BURIED IN HELL

The book Zohar, III, (282), tells us that Jesus died like a beast and was buried in that "dirt heap...where they throw the dead bodies of dogs and asses, and where the sons of Esau [the Christians] and of Ismael [the Turks], also Jesus and Mahommed, uncircumcized and unclean like dead dogs, are buried."

9. WORSHIPPED AS GOD AFTER HIS DEATH BY HIS FOLLOWERS
George El. Edzard, in his book *Avoda Sara,* quotes the following words of the commentator on the *Hilkoth Akum* (V,3) of Maimonides:

"In many passages of the Talmud mention is made of Jesus the Nazarene and of his disciples, and that the Gentiles believe that there is no other God besides him. In the book *Chizzuk Emunah,* part I, ch. 36, we read: "The Christians build up an argument from this [Zachary XII, 10] and say: Behold how thew Prophet testified that in future ages the Jews would would lament and weep because they crucified and killed the Messiah who was sent to them; and to prove that he meant Jesus the Nazarene, possessing both the divine and human nature, they quote the words: *And they looked upon him whom they transfixed and they wept over him as a mother over her first born child.""* Maimonides attempts to prove how much Christians err in worshipping Jesus in his book *Hilkoth Melakhim* (IX, 4):

"If all the things he did had prospered, if he had rebuilt the Sanctuary in its place, and had gathered together the dispersed tribes of Israel, then he would certainly be the Messiah....But if so far hew has not done so and if he was killed, then it is clear he was not the Messiah whom the Law tells us to expect. He was similar to all the good and upright rulers of the House of David who died, and whom the Holy and Blessed Lord raised up for no other reason but to prove to many, as it is said (in Dan. XI, 35): *And some of them who understand shall fall, to try and to purge them and to make them white, even till the end of time, because the appointed time is not yet.* Daniel also prophesised about Jesus the Nazarene who thought he was the Christ, and who was put to death by the judgment of the Senate: (Dan. V.14): *...and the robbers of thy people shall exalt*

*themselves to establish the vision; but they shall fail.* What could be plainer? For all the Prophets said that the Christ would set Israel free, would bring it salvation, restore its dispersed peoples and confirm their laws. But he was the cause of the destruction of Israel and caused the rest of them to be dispersed and humiliated, so that the Law was changed and the greater part of the world was seduced to worship another God. Truly no one can understand the designs of the Creator, nor are his ways our ways. For all that has been built up by Jesus the Nazarene, and by the Turks who came after him, tend only to prepare the way for the coming of Christ the King, and to prepare the whole world equally for the service of the Lord, as it is said: *For then I shall give a clean moth to all peoples that all may call upon the name of the Lord, and bow down in unison before him.* How is this being accomplished? Already the whole world is filled with the praise of Christ, the Law and the Commandments, and his praises have spread to far distant lands and to peoples whose hearts and bodies are uncircumcized. These discuss with one another about the Law that was destroyed - some saying that the commandments were once true, but have ceased to exist; others that there is a great mystery about it, that the Messiah-King has come and that their doctrine has revealed it.

But when the Christ truly comes and is successful, and is raised up and exalted, then everything will be changed and these things will be shown to be false and vain."

10. AN IDOL

In the Tract *Abhodah Zarah,* (21a *Toseph),* we read:

"It is of importance to inquire the reasons why men nowadays even sell and rent their houses to Gentiles. Some say this is legal because it is said in *Tosephta:* No one shall rent his house to a gentile either here [in the land of Israel] or elsewhere because it is known that he will bring an idol into it. It is nevertheless allowed to rent them stables, barns and lodging houses, even though it is known that they will bring idols into them. The reason is because a distinction can be made between a place into which an idol will be carried in order to leave it there permanently, and a place where it will not be left permanently, in which case it is allowed. And since the gentiles, among whom we now live, do not bring their idol into their homes to leave it there permanently, but only for a time - while someone is dead in the house or when someone is dying, nor do they even perform any religious rites there - it is therefore permitted to sell and rent them houses."

Rabbi Ascher, in his Commentary on *Abhodah Zarah* (83d) speaks not less clearly on this matter: "Today it is permitted to rent houses to Gentiles because they bring their idol into them only for a time, when somebody is sick." And in the same place he says "Today they have a practice of incensing their idol.""

All this, and much more like it, proves beyond a doubt that when the Rabbis speak of the idols of the Gentiles among whom they lived at that time, when no idols were worshipped, they clearly meant the Christian "idol," namely, the image of Christ on the crucifix and the Holy Communion.

**Note About The Cross**

In Jewish writings there is no directly corresponding word for the Christian Cross. The cross T on which those condemned to death were crucified, was called *Tau* by the Phoenicians and the Hebrews, and this name and sign for it was afterwards taken over into the alphabet of the Jews and of the Greeks and the Romans. The Cross honored by the Christians, however, is called by the following names:

1. *Tsurath Haattalui* - the image who was hanged.

2. *Elil* - vanity, idol.

3. *Tselem* - image. Hence the Crusaders in Jewish books are called *Tsalmerim* (ein Tsalmer)

4. *Scheti Veerebh* - warp and woof, which is taken from the textile art.

5. *Kokhabh* - star; on account of the four rays emanating from it.

6. *Pesila* - a sculpture, a carven idol.

But whenever it is mentioned it is always in the sense of an idol or of something despicable, as can be seen from the following quotations: In *Orach Chaiim,* 113,8:

"If a Jew when praying should meet a Christian [*Akum*] carrying a *star* [a crucifix] in his hand, even if he has come to a place in his prayer where it is necessary to bow down to worship God in his heart, he must not to so lest he should seem to bow down before an image."

In *Iore Dea,* 150,2:

"Even if a Jew should get a splinter in his foot in front of an idol, or if he should drop his money before it, he must not stoop down to remove the splinter or to gather his money lest he should seem to adore it. But he should either sit down or turn his back or his side to the idol and then remove the splinter."

But whenever it is not possible for a Jew to turn away like this, the following rule must be observed (in *Iore Dea,* 3, *Hagah):*

"It is not permitted to bow down or to remove one's hat before princes or priests who wear a cross on their dress, as is their custom. Care must be taken, however, not to be noticed in failing to do so. For instance, one can throw some coins on the ground and stoop down to pick them up before they pass by. In this way it is permitted to bow down or to remove one's hat before them." A distinction is also made between a cross which is venerated and a cross which is worn around the neck as a souvenir or as an ornament. The former is to be regarded as an idol, but not necessarily the latter. In *Iore Dea,* 141, 1,*Hagah,* it says:

"The image of a cross, before which they bow down, is to be treated as an idol, and it is not to be used until it is destroyed. However, a 'warp and woof' if hung around the neck as a souvenir is not to be regarded as an idol and can be used."

The sign of the cross made with the hand, by which Christians are wont to bless themselves, is called in Jewish "the moving of the fingers here and there" (hinc et hinc).

**Article III. - The Teachings of Christ**

The Seducer and Idolator could teach nothing but falsehood and heresy which was irrational and impossible to observe.

1. FALSHOOD

In *Abhodah Zarah* (6a) it says:

"A Nazarene is one who follows the false teachings of that man who taught them to worship on the first day of the Sabbath."

2. HERESY

In the same book *Abohah Zar.* (Ch.I, 17a *Toseph)* mention is made of the heresy of James. A little further on (27b) we learn that this James was noneother than the disciple of Jesus:"

...James Sekhanites, one of the disciples of Jesus, of whom we spoke in chapter 1."
But James taught, not his own doctrine, but that of Jesus.

3. IMPOSSIBLE TO OBSERVE

The author of *Nizzachon* argues as follows on this point:

"A written law of the Christians is: If a Jew strike you on one cheek, turn the other also to him and do not in any way return the blow.And ch. VI, v. 27 says: *Love your enemies; do good to them who hate you; bless them who curse you and pray for those who do you harm; unto him who strikes you on one cheek offer him the other. To him who takes away thy cloak do not forbid him to take thy coat also,* etc. The same is found in Matthew ch. V, v.39. But I have never seen any Christian keep this law, nor did Jesus himself behave as he taught others to do. For we find in *John* ch XVIII, v22, that when someone struck him on the face, he did not turn the other cheek, but became angry on account of this one stroke and asked "Why do you strike me"? Likewise in the *Acts of the Apostles,* ch.XXIII, v. 3, we read: that when the High Priest ordered them that stood by to strike him on the mouth, Paul did not turn the other cheek; he cursed him saying "God shall smite thee thou whited wall, etc." This is contrary to their beliefs and destroys the foundation upon which their religion rests, for they boast that the law of Jesus is easy to observe. If Paul himself, who may be called the Dispenser of Jesus, could not preserve the precept of Jesus, who among the others who believe in him can prove to me that he can do so?"

The author, however, who had the Gospels and the Acts of the Apostles under his hand, could not have failed to understand in what sense Christ commanded his followers to turn the other cheek to him who would strike them, since in another place he commanded his followers to cut off a hand or an arm, and to pluck out an eye if these should scandalize them. No one who has had the least acquaintance with the Holy Scriptures ever thought that these commands should be taken literally. Only deep malice and ignorance of the times in which Jesus lived can explain why the Jews, even to this day, use these passages to detract from the teachings of Jesus Christ.

# CHAPTER II

# CHRISTIANS IN THE TALMUD

There are three things to be considered in this chapter:

1. The names by which Christians are called in the Talmud.
2. What kind of people the Talmud pictures Christians to be.
3. What the Talmud says about the religious worship of the Christians.

### Article I. - The Names Given to Christians in the Talmud

As in our languages Christians take their name from Christ, so in the language of the Talmud Christians are called *Notsrim,* from Jesus the Nazarene. But Christians are also called by the names used in the Talmud to designate all non-Jews: *Abhodah Zarah, Akum, Obhde Elilim, Minim, Nokhrim, Edom, Amme Haarets, Goim, Apikorosim, Kuthrim.*

1. *Abhodah Zarah* - Strange worship, idolatry. The Talmudic Tract on Idolatry is thus entitled: *Obhde Abhodah Zarah* - Idol Worshippers. That *Abhodah Zarah* really means the cult of idols is clear from the Talmud itself: "Let Nimrod come and testify that Abraham was not a server of *Abhodah Zarah* ." But in these days of Abraham there existed no strange cult either of the Turks or the Nazarenes, but only the worship of the true God and idolatry. In *Schabbath* (ibid. 82a), it says:

"Rabbi Akibah says: How do we know that *Abhodah Zarah,* like an unclean woman, contaminates those who subscribe to it? Because Isaiah says: *Thou shalt cast them away like a menstruation cloth; and shalt say unto it, Get thee hence."*

In the first part of this verse mention is made of idols made from gold and silver.

The learned Maimonides also clearly demonstrates that the Jews regarded Christians as *Abhodah Zarah*. In *Perusch* (78c) he says: "And be it known that Christian people who follow Jesus, although their teachings vary, are all worshippers of idols (*Abhodah Zarah*)."

2. *Akum* - This word is made up of the initial letters of the words *Obhde Kokhabkim U Mazzaloth* - worshippers of stars and planets. It was thus that the Jews formerly styled the Gentiles who lacked all knowledge of the true God. Now, however, the word *Akum* in Jewish books, especially in the *Schulkhan Arukh,* is applied to Christians. This is evident from numerous passages:

In the *Orach Chaiim* (113,8) those who use a cross are called *Akum.* In the *Iore Dea* (148, 5, 12), those who celebrate the feasts of Christmas and New Year, eight days afterwards, are called worshippers of the stars and planets: "Thus if a gift is sent to the *Akum,* even in these times, on the eighth day after Christmas, which they call the New Year," etc.

3. *Obhde Elilim* - Servers of idols. This name has the same meaning as *Akum.* Non-Jews are frequently called by this name. In the *Orach Chaiim,* for example (215, 5), it says: "A blessing should not be pronounced over incense which belongs to the servers of idols."

But at the same time when the *Schulkhan Arukh* was written there were no worshippers of the stars and planets (*Akum*); there were no 'servers of idols' among those who lived with the Jews. Thus, for example, the author of the Commentary on the *Schulkhan Arukh* (entitled *Magen Abraham),* Rabbi Calissensis who died in Poland in 1775, in note 8, on No. 244 of the *Orach Chaiim* (where it is allowed to finish a work on the Sabbath with the help of an *Akum)* says: "Here in our city the question is raised about the price of hiring worshippers of the stars and planets who sweep the public streets when they work on the Sabbath."

4. *Minim* - Heretics. In the Talmud those who possess books called the Gospels are heretics. Thus in *Schabbath* (116a) it says: "Rabbi Meir calls the books of the *Minim Aven Gilaion* [iniquitous volumes] because they call them Gospels."

5. *Edom* - Edomites. Rabbi Aben Ezra, when he speaks about the Emperor Constantine who changed his religion and placed the image of him who was hanged on his banner, adds: "Rome therefore is called the Kingdom of the Edomites."

And Rabbi Bechai, in his *Kad Hakkemach* (*fol.* 20a, on *Isaiah,* ch. LXVI, 17) writes:

"They are called Edomites who move their fingers 'here and there'" (who make the sign of the cross).

Likewise Rabbi Bechai, commenting on the words of Isaiah *(loc. cit.),* "those who eat the flesh of swine" adds: "These are the Edomites." Rabbi Kimchi, however, calls them "Christians." And Rabbi Abarbinel, in his work *Maschima Ieschua* (36d) says: "The Nazarenes are Romans, the sons of Edom."

6. *Goi* - Race, or people. The Jews also call a man a Goi - a gentile; they call a gentile woman a *Goiah.* Sometimes, but very rarely, Israelites are called by this name. It is mostly applied to non-Jews, or idolators. In Jewish books which treat of Idolatry, worshippers of idols are often called by this single word *Goi.* For this reason, in more recent editions of the Talmud the use of the word *Goi* is purposely avoided and other words for non-Jews are substituted.

It is well known that in the Jewish language, the Jews call Christians among whom they live, *Goim.* Nor do the Jews deny this. Sometimes in their popular magazines they say that this word means nothing harmful or evil. But the contrary can be seen in their books written in the Hebrew language. For instance, in *Choschen Hammischpat* (34, 22), the name *Goi* is used in a depraved sense:

"Traitors and Epicureans and Apostates are worse than *Goim"*

7. *Nokhtrim* - strangers, foreigners. This name is used for all who are not Jews, and therefor for Christians.

8. *Amme Haarets* - People of the earth, idiots. There are some who say that people of other races are not meant by this, but only crude and uneducated people. There are passages, however, which leave no doubt about the matter. In the Holy Scripture, Book of Esra, ch. X, 2, we read: *We have sinned against our God, and have taken strange wives [nokhrioth] of the people of the earth.* That *people of the earth* denotes idolators is clear from *Zohar,* I, 25a: “The People of the earth - *Obhde Abhodah Zarah*, idolaters.

9. *Basar Vedam* - Flesh and blood; carnal men who are destined to perdition and who can have no communion with God. That Christians are *flesh and blood*, is proved from the prayer book:

"Whoever meets a wise and educated Christian can say: Blessed art thou O Lord, King of the Universe, who dispenseth of thy wisdom to Flesh and Blood," etc.

Likewise in another prayer, in which they ask God soon to restore the kingdom of David and to send Elias and the Messia, etc., they aak him to take away their poverty so that they will have no need to accept gifts from “flesh and blood,” nor to trade with them, nor to seek wages from them.

10. *Apikorosim* - Epicureans. All are called by this name who do not observe God’s precepts, as well as all those, even Jews themselves, who express private judgments in matters of faith. How much more, therefore, Christians!

11. *Kuthim* - Samaritans. But since there are no longer any Samaritans, and since there are many references in recent Jewish books to Samaritans, who can doubt that this does not mean the Christians?

Furthermore, in this matter of naming those who are not Jews, it is to be particularly noted that Jewish writings apply these names indiscriminately and promiscuously when they speak of the same thing, and almost in the same words. For instance, in the Tract *Abhodah Zarah* (25b) the word Goi is employed, but in the *Schulkhan Arukh (Iore Dea* 153, 2) *Akum* is used. *Kerithuth* (6b) uses *Goim*; *Jebhammoth* (61a) uses *Akum*; *Abhodah Zar.* (2a) uses *Obhde Elilim; Thoseph* uses *Goim* and *Obhde Ab., Choschen Ham (*Venetian ed.) uses *Kuthi;* (Slav. ed.) *Akum.* And many more instances could be quoted.

Maimonides in his book on Idolatry indiscriminately calls all the following idolators: *Goim, Akum, Obhde Kokhabhim, Obhde Elilim,* etc.

**Article II. - What the Talmud Teaches About Christians**

In the preceding chapter we saw what the Jews think of the Founder of the Christian religion, and how much they despise his name. This being so, it would not be expected that they would have any better opinion about those who follow Jesus the Nazarene. In fact, nothing more abominable can be imagined than what they have to say about Christians. They say that they are idolaters, the worst kind of people, much worse than the Turks, murderers, fornicators, impure animals, like dirt, unworthy to be called men, beasts in human form, worthy of the name of beasts, cows, asses, pigs, dogs, worse than dogs; that they propagate after the manner of beasts, that they have diabolic origin, that their souls come from the devil and return to the devil in hell after death; and that even the body of a dead Christian is nothing different from that of an animal.

1. IDOLATERS

Since Christians follow the teachings of *that man*, whom the Jews regard as a Seducer and an Idolater, and since they worship him as God, it clearly follows that they merit the name of idolater, in no way different from those among whom the Jews lived before the birth of Christ, and whom they taught should be exterminated by every possible means.

This is best demonstrated by the names they give Christians, and by the unmistakable words of Maimonides which prove that all who bear the name of Christian are idolaters. And anyone who examines Jewish books which speak of the "Worshippers of the Stars and Planets," "Epicureans," "Samaritans," etc., cannot but conclude that these idolaters are none other than Christians. The Turks are always called "Ismaelites," never idolaters.

2. CHRISTIANS WORSE THAN THE TURKS

Maimonides in *Hilkoth Maakhaloth* (ch.IX) says:

"It is not permitted to drink the wine of a stranger who becomes a convert, that is, one who accepts the seven precepts of Noah, but is permitted to gain some benefit from it. It is allowed to leave wine alone with him, but not to place it before him. The same is permitted in the case of all gentiles who are not idolaters, such as the Turks [Ismaelites]. A Jew, however, is not permitted to drink their wine, although he may use it to his own advantage."

3. MURDERERS

In *Abhodah Zarah* (22a) it says:

"A Jew must not associate himself with gentiles because they are given to the shedding of blood."

Likewise in *Iore Dea* (153, 2):

"An Israelite must not associate himself with the *Akum* [Christians] because they are given to the shedding of blood."

In the *Abhodah Zarah* (25b) it says:

"The Rabbis taught: If a Goi joins an Israelite on the road, he [the Jew] should walk on his right side. Rabbi Ismael, the son of Rabbi Jochanan the nephew of Beruka, says: if he carries a sword, let the Jew walk on his right side. If the *Goi* carries a stick, the Jew should walk on his left side. If he is climbing a hill or descending a steep incline, the Jew must not go in front with the Goi behind, but the Jew must go behind and the *Goi* in front, nor must he stoop down in front of him for fear the Goi might crack his skull. And if he should ask the Jew how far he is going, he should pretend he is going a long way, as Jacob our Father said to the impious Esau: *until I come to my Lord in Seir (Gen. XXXIII, 14-17),* but it adds: *Jacob set out for Sukoth."*

In *Orach Chaiim* (20, 2) it says:

"Do not sell your overcoat (*Talith)* with the fringes to an Akum, lest he should join up with a Jew on the road and kill him. It is also forbidden to exchange or lend your overcoat with a Gentile, except for a short time and when there is nothing to be feared from him."

4. FORNICATORS

In the *Abhodah Zarah* (15b) it says:

"Animals of the masculine sex must not be left in the barns of the Gentiles with their men, nor animals of the feminine sex with their women; much less must animals of the feminine sex be left with their men and of the masculine sex with their women. Nor must sheep be left to the care of their shepherds; nor must any intercourse be had with them; nor must children be given into their care to learn to read or to learn a trade."

In the same tract a little farther on (22a) it is explained why animals must not be allowed in the barns of Gentiles, and why Jews are not permitted to have sexual intercourse with them:

"Animals must not be allowed to go near the *Goim,* because they are suspected of having intercourse with them. Nor must women cohabit with them because they are over-sexed."

In fol. 22b of the same book the reason is given why animals especially of the feminine sex must be kept away from their women: "...because when Gentile men come to their neighbors' houses to commit adultery with their wives and do not find them at home, they fornicate with the sheep in the barns instead. And sometimes even when their neighbors' wives are at home, they prefer to fornicate with the animals; for they love the sheep of the Israelites more than their own women."

It is for the same reason that animals are not to be entrusted to Goi shepherds, nor children to their educators.

5. UNCLEAN

The Talmud gives two reasons why the *Goim* are unclean: because they eat unclean things, and because they themselves have not been cleansed (from original sin) on Mount Sinai. In *Schabbath,* (145b) it says:

"Why are the *Goim* unclean? Because they eat abominable things and animals that crawl on their belly."

Likewise in *Abhodah Zarah*, 22b:

"Why are the Goim unclean? Because they were not present at Mount Sinai. For when the serpent entered into Eve he infused her with uncleanness. But the Jews were cleansed from this when they stood on Mount Sinai; the *Goim,* however, who were not on Mount Sinaim were not cleansed."

6. COMPARED TO DUNG

"When ten persons are praying together in one place and they say *Kaddisch,* or *Kedoschah,* anyone, even though he does not belong there, may respond Amen. There are some, however, who say that no *dung* or *Akum* must be present."

In *Iore Dea* (198, 48) *Hagah*, it says:

"When Jewish women come out of a bath they must take care to meet a friend first, and not something unclean or a Chrsitian. For if so, a woman, if she wants to keep holy, should go back and bathe again."

It is worthy of note that the following list of unclean things is a given in*Biur Hetib*, a commentary on the *Schulchan Arukh*:

"A woman must wash herself again if she sees any unclean things, such as a dog, an ass, or People of the Earth; a Christian (*Akum*), a camel, a pig, a horse, and a leper.

7. NOT LIKE MEN, BUT BEASTS

In *Kerithuth* (6b p. 78) it says:

"The teaching of the Rabbis is: He who pours oil over a *Goi,* and over dead bodies is freed from punishment. This is true for an animal because it is not a man. But how can it be said that by pouring oil over a *Goi* one is freed from punishment, since a *Goi* is also a man? But this is not true, for it is written: *Ye are my flock, the flock of my pasture are men (Ezechiel, XXXIV, 31).* You are thus called men, but the Goim are not called men." In the Tract *Makkoth* (7b) he is said to be guilty of killing "except when, if intending to kill an animal he kills a man by mistake, or intending to kill a *Goi,* he kills an Israelite."

In *Orach Chaiim* (225, 10) it says:

"He who sees beautiful creatures, even though it be an Akum or an animal, let him say 'Blessed art thou Our Lord God, King of the Universe, who has placed such things on the earth!'"

8. THEY DIFFER ONLY IN FORM FROM BEASTS

In *Midrasch Talpioth* (fol. 225d) it says:

"God created them in the form of men for the glory of Israel. But *Akum* were created for the sole end of ministering unto them [the Jews] day and night. Nor can they ever be relieved from this service. It is becoming to the son of a king [an Israelite] that animals in their natural form, and animals in the form of human beings should minister unto him."

We can quote here also what is said in *Orach Chaiim,* 57, 6a:

"If pigs are to be pitied when they suffer from disease, because their intestines are similar to ours, how much more should the *Akum* be pitied when thus affected."

9. ANIMALS

In Zohar, II, (64b) it says:

"...People who worship idols, and who are called cow and ass, as it is written: I have a cow and an ass..."

Rabbi Bechai, in his book *Kad Hakkemach*, ch. I, beginning with the word Geulah - redemption - referring to *Psalm* 80, v.13:

*The boar out of the wood doth waste it,* says:

"The letter *ain* is dropped [suspended] the same as these worshippers are followers of him who was suspended."

Buxtorf (*Lex.*) says:

"By *wild pig* the author here means the Christians who eat pork and, like pigs, have destroyed the vineyard of Israel, the City of Jerusalem, and who believe in the 'suspended' Christ. Else the letter ain is dropped in this word because they, as worshippers of Christ who was hanged, are also dropped."

Rabbi Edels, in commenting on *Kethuboth* (110b) says:

"The Psalmist compares the *Akum* to the unclean beast in the woods."

10. WORSE THAN ANIMALS

Rabbi Schelomo Iarchi (Raschi), famous Jewish commentator, explaining the law of Moses (*Deuter.* XIV, 21) forbidding the eating of meat of wounded animals, but which must be given to the 'stranger in thy gates,' or which, according to *Exodus* (XXII, 30) is to be thrown to the dogs, has this to say:

"...for he is like a dog. Are we to take to word 'dog' here literally? By no means. For the text in speaking of dead bodies says, *Or thou mayest sell it to an alien.* This applies much more to the meat of wounded animals, for which it is permitted to accept payment. Why therefore does the Scripture say it may be thrown to 'dogs?' In order to teach you that a dog is to be more respected than the *Nokhri.*"

11. THEY PROPAGATE LIKE BEASTS

In the *Sanhedrin* (74b) *Tosephoth,* it says:

"The sexual intercourse of a *Goi* is like that of a beast."

And in *Kethuboth* (3b) it says:

"The seed of a *Goi* is worth the same as that of a beast."

Hence it is to be inferred that Christian marriage is not true marriage.

In *Kidduschim* (68a), it says:

"...How do we know this? Rabbi Huna says: You can read: Remain here with the ass, that is, with a people like an ass. Hence it appears that they are not capable of contracting marriage."

And in *Eben Haezer* (44, 8):

"If a Jew enters into marriage with an *Akum* (Christian), or with his servant, the marriage is null. For they are not capable of entering into matrimony. Likewise if an *Akum*or a servant enter into matrimony with a Jew, the marriage is null."

In *Zohar* (II, 64b) it says:

"Rabbi Abba says: If only idolaters alone had sexual intercourse, the world would not continue to exist. Hence we are taught that a Jew should not give way to those infamous robbers. For if these propagate in greater numbers, it will be impossible for us to continue to exist because of them. For they give birth to sucklings the same as dogs."

12. CHILDREN OF THE DEVIL

In *Zohar* (I, 28b) we read:

*"Now the serpent was more subtle than any beast of the field, etc.* (*Genes.* III, 1.) 'More subtle' that is towards evil; 'than all beasts' that is, the idolatrous people of the earth.

For they are the children of the ancient serpent which seduced Eve."

The best argument used by the Jews to prove that Christians are of the race of the devil is the fact that they are uncircumcized. The foreskin on non-Jews prevents them from being called the children of the Most High God. For by circumcision the name of God - *Schaddai* - is complete in the flesh of a circumcized Jew. The form of the letter *Isch* is in his nostrils, the letter *Daleth* in his (bent) arm, and ain appears in his sexual organ by circumcision. In non-circumcized gentiles, therefore, such as Christians, there are only two letters, *Isch* and *Daleth,* which make the word *Sched,* which means devil. They are, therefore, children of the *Sched,* the devil.

13. THE SOULS OF CHRISTIANS ARE EVIL AND UNCLEAN

The teaching of the Jews is that God created two natures, one good and the other evil, or one nature with two sides, one clean and the other unclean. From the unclean side, called *Keliphah* - rind, or scabby crust - the souls of Christians are said to have come.

In *Zohar* (I, 131a) it says:

"idolatrous people, however, since they exist, befoul the world, because their souls come out of the unclean side."

And in *Emek Hammelech* (23d) it says:

"The souls of the impious come from *Keliphah,* which is death and the shadows of death."

*Zohar* (I, 46b, 47a) goes to show that this unclean side is the left side, from which the souls of the Christians come:

*"And he created every living thing,* that is, the Israelites, because they are the children of the Most High God, and their holy souls come out from Him. But where do the souls of the idolatrous gentiles come from? Rabbi Eliezer says: from the left side, which makes their souls unclean. They are therefore all unclean and they pollute all who come in contact with them."

14. AFTER DEATH THEY GO DOWN TO HELL

The Elders teach that Abraham sits at the gate of Gehenna and prevents any circumcized person from entering there; but that all the uncircumcized go down to hell.

In *Rosch Haschanach* (17a) it says:

"Heretics and Epicureans and Traitors go down into hell."

15. THE FATE OF DEAD CHRISTIANS

The bodies of Christians after death are called by the odious name of *Pegarim,* which is the word used in Holy Scripture for the dead bodies of the damned and of animals, but never for the pious dead who are called *Metim.* Thus the *Schulchan Arukh* orders that a dead Christian must be spoken of in the same way as a dead animal.

In *Iore Dea* (377, 1) it says:

"Condolences must not be offered to anyone on account of the death of his servants or handmaids. All that may be said is 'May God restore your lost one, the same as we say to a man who has lost a cow or an ass.'"

Nor must Christians be avoided for seven days after they have buried someone, as the law of Moses commands, since they are not men; for the burial of an animal does not pollute one.

In *Iebhammoth* (61a) it says:

"The *Nokhrim* are not rendered unclean by a burial. For it is said: *Ye are my sheep, the sheep of my pasture; ye are men.* You are thus called men, but not the *Nokhrim."*

**Article III. - About Christian Rites and Worship**

Since Christians are regarded by the Jews as idolators, all their forms of worship are idolatrous. Their priests are called priests of Baal; their temples are called houses of lies and idolatry, and everything they contain, such as chalices, statues and books, are regarded as made for the serving of idols; their prayers, both private and public, are sinful and offensive to God; and their festivals are called days of evil.

1. PRIESTS

The Talmud speaks of priests, the ministers of Christian worship, as idolatrous and belonging to the god Baal. They are also called *Komarim* - Soothsayers; and also *Galachim,* the shaved, because they shave their heads, particularly the monks.

In *Abhodah Zarah* (14b) *Toseph,* it says:

"It is forbidden to sell books of the prophets to the soothsayers, since they may use them for their evil worship in their idolatrous temples. Those who do so sin against the law which forbids us to place an obstacle in the way of a blind person. It is also forbidden to sell them to a Christian who is not shaved, for he is sure to give or sell them to one of them who is shaved."

2. CHRISTIAN CHURCHES

A place of Christian worship is called (1) *Beth Tilfah,* a house of vanity and foolishness, in place of *Beth Tefilah,* a house of prayer; (2) *Beth Abhodha Zarah,* a House of Idolatry; (3) *Beth Hatturapi Schel Letsim,* a house of Evil Laughter.

In *Abhodah Zarah* (78) the Perusch of Maimonides, it says:

"Be it known to you that it is beyond a doubt forbidden by law to pass through a Christian city in which there is a house of vanity, that is, a house of idolatry; much more to live therein. But we today, as punishment for our sins, are subject to them, and are forced to live in their countries, as it was foretold in *Deuteronomy* (IV, 28): *And there ye shall serve gods, the work of men's hands, of wood and stone...*Thus if it is allowed as predicted to pass around a Christian city, much more so must we pass around an idolatrous temple; nor is it allowed us even to look inside and above all to enter in."

A Jew is forbidden not only to enter a Christian church, but even to go near it, except under certain circumstances.

In *Iore Dea* (142, 10) it says:

"It is forbidden to stand in the shadow of a house of idolatry, whether from the inside or the outside, for a distance of four cubits from the front door. It is not forbidden, however, to stand under the shadows of the back of a church. Nor is the shadow forbidden us if the church stands in a place where formerly there was public road, which was taken from the community and the house of idolatry built upon it. For the road is still there. But if the house of idolatry existed before the road, it is not permitted to pass before it. There are some who say that it is forbidden to pass there in any case."

Neither is a Jew allowed to listen to, or admire the beautiful music of the churches.

In *Iore Dea* (142, 15) it says:

"It is forbidden to listen to the music if idolatrous worship, and to examine the statues of their idols; for even by looking at them one can be influenced by the evil of idolatry. But one can look who does not intend to be so affected." Likewise a Jew is not allowed to have a house near a church; nor is he allowed to rebuild a house which has been destroyed in such a place. In *Iore Dea* (143, 1) it says:

"If a house near an idolatrous temple belonging to the *Akum* falls down, it must not be rebuilt. A Jew must remove it a certain distance away if he wishes to rebuild it. But he must fill up the vacant space between his house and the church with bushes and rubbish so that the space will not be used to extend the idolatrous temple."

Here may be added what a certain Rabbi Kelomimus said about a Christian church (in the book *Nizzachon)* to the Emperor Henry III, who gave him permission to speak his opinion freely about the Basilica which he had recently built at Spires:

"After the Emperor Henry III, a very wicked man, had completed the building of that "Abyss," he sent for Rabbi Kelominus and said to him: "I want to ask you, how does this Basilica which I have built compare with the magnificence of Solomon's Temple, about which so many volumes have been written?" He replied: 'My Lord, if you will permit me that you will let me go unharmed, I will tell you the truth about it.' The Emperor answered: 'I give you my word as a lover of the truth and as an Emperor, that no harm shall come to you.' Then the Jew said: 'If you gathered together all you have spent so far, and added to it all the silver and gold in your treasury, it would not suffice even to pay the workmen and craftsmen that Solomon employed; for it is written *(Chron.* II, ch 2): *And Solomon told out threescore and ten thousand men to bear burdens, and fourscore thousand to hew in the mountains, and three thousand and six hundred to oversee them.* Eight years were spent in the building of the Temple, much more than you spent in building this *Tehon* [Abyss]. And when Solomon had finished his Temple, see what the Scripture says about it: *The priests could not stand to minister by reason of the cloud; for the glory of God had filled the House of the Lord (Chron.* II, Ch. 5, 14). But if someone loaded an ass with putrid garbage and led it into this abyss of yours, no one would notice the difference!' The Emperor Henry then replied: 'Were it not that I have sworn to let you go unharmed, I would order your head cut off.'"

3. CHALICES

Chalises used in the Sacrifice of the mass are spoken of as vessels in which filth is offered up to the idol. Moses Kozzensis, in *Hilkoth Abhodah Zarah* (10b) says:

"A Jew who buys Chalises of the Goi, which are broken and thrown away, it is not permitted to sell them again to them, because their priest of Baal will use them in the worship of the idol."

4. BOOKS

The Talmud calls the books of the Christians *Minim* - heretical books - *Siphre Debeth Abidan* - Books of the House of Perdition. The Talmud in particular speaks of the books of the Gospels. Thus in *Schabbath* (116a) *Toseph:*

"Rabbi Meir calls heretical books *Aaven Gilaion* (volumes of iniquity) because the call them Gospels."

And Rabbi Jochanan calls these books *Aavon Gilaion,* evil books. The *Schulchan Arukh,* Crakow edition, gives this name as Aven Niktabh al Haggilaion - iniquity written in a book.

Buxtorf says: "In the Arukh there is a note *Scheker Niktabh al Gilaion,* which means, a lie written in a book."

All the Talmudists agree that the books of the Christians should be destroyed. They differ only as to what should be done with the names of God contained in them.

In *Schabbath* (116a) it says:

"The Glossaries of our own books and the books of the heretics are not to be saved from the flames, if they should catch fire on the Sabbath day. Rabbi Jose, however, says: 'On festival days the divine names should be torn out of the books of the Christians and hidden away; what remains must be given to the flames.' But Rabbi Tarphon says: 'In order that I may be remembered by my children, if those books should ever fall into my hands I would burn them together with the divine names contained therein. For if one is chased by an assassin, or by a serpent, it would be better to take refuge in a pagan temple than in one of theirs; because the Christians knowingly resist the truth, whereas the pagans do so unknowingly."

5. PRAYERS

Christian prayers are called, not *Tefillah,* but *Tiflah.* They change the point and insert *Iod* which makes it read to mean sin, foolishness and transgression.

6. CHRISTIAN FESTIVALS

Christian festivals, especially Sunday, are called *Ion Ed* - day of destruction, perdition, misfortune or calamity. They are also simply called *Iom Notsri* - Christian Days. The word *Ed* rightly interpreted means misfortune or calamity, as appears from the *Gemarah* and the Glossaries of Maimonides in *Abhodah Zarah* (2a):

"The word *Edehem* means the festivals of the Christians, since it is written (in Deuter. XXXII, 35): *the day of their calamity*."

Maimonides also says in *Abhodah Zarah* (78c):

"The words *Edehem* means the foolishness of their festivlas. It is the name for their despicable feast days which do not merit the name of *Moedim*, for they are really vain and evil."

Baretenora also writes:

"The word *Edehem* is the name for their ignominious festivals and solemnities."

The marginal notes of *Tosephtoth* also give this name to Christian festivals. Thus in *Abhodah Zarah* (6a):

"The Day of Evil, that is the Christian Day, is forbidden to us as well as all their other feast days."

Some Christian festivals are mentioned by name, such as the feast of Christmas and Easter. Moses Mikkozzi, referring to the above text of *Abhodah Zarah* , says:

"Rabbi Sammuel declares, in the name of Solomon Iarchi, that in particular the festivals of Christmas and Easter, which are their principal *evil* days and the foundation of their religion, are forbidden to us."

Maimonides, in *hilkoth Akum* (ch. IX) has the same: "Sammuel repeats the words of Rabbi Sal. Iarchi which forbid us particularly to celebrate the feasts of Christmas and Easter, which are celebrated on account of him who was hanged."

Furthermore, indications of the impiety of the Jews are to be found in the names which they give to these Christian festivals: For in place of using *Tav* in the word *Nithal,* they often write *Tet* and call it *Nital* for the Latin word *Natalis,* the Feast of the Nativity. They make it appear as if this word were from the root Natal which connotes extermination or destruction. Likewise they refuse to use the word *Paschal (Pesach)* for the Christian feast of Easter. The substitute *Koph* for *Phe* and insert the letter *iod* and call it *Ketsach* or *Kesach.* Both pronunciations have an evil meaning. *Ketsach* is from the root *Katsah,* meaning to amputate or cut off from, and *Kesach* is from the root *Kesa,* meaning to wood or a gallows. This is done because the feast of Easter is celebrated by Christians in memory of Christ - the one who was hanged - who was put to death and who rose again from the dead.

# PART TWO

# PRECEPTS OF THE TALMUD

## CONCERNING CHRISTIANS

From what has been shown thus far, it is clear that, according to the teaching of the Talmud, Christians are idolaters and hateful to Jews. As a consequence, every Jew who wishes to please God has a duty to observe all the precepts which were given to the Fathers of their race when they lived in the Holy Land concerning the idolatrous gentiles, both those who lived amongst them and those in nearby countries.

A Jew is therefore required to (1) To avoid Christians; (2) To do all he can to exterminate them.

# CHAPTER I

# CHRISTIANS MUST BE AVOIDED

Jews are required to avoid all contact with Christians for four reasons: (1) Because they are not worthy to share in the Jewish way of life; (2) Because they are unclean; (3) Because they are idolators; (4) Because they are murderers.

**Article I. - Christians Must Be Avoided - Because They Are Unworthy to Share Jewish Customs**

A Jew, by the fact that he belongs to the chosen people and is circumcized, possesses so great a dignity that no one, not even an angel, can share equality with him. In fact, he is considered almost the equal of God. "He who strikes an Israelite" says Rabbi Chanina "acts as if he slaps the face of God's Divine Majesty."

A Jew is always considered good, in spite of certain sins which he may commit; nor can his sins contaminate him, any more

Than dirt contaminates the kernel in a nut, but only soils its shell. A Jew alone is looked upon as a man; the whole world is his and all things should serve him, especially "animals which have the form of men."

Thus it is plain that they regard all contact with Christians as contaminating and as detracting from their dignity. They are therefore required to keep as far away as possible from all who live and act as Christians do.

1. A JEW MUST NOT SALUTE A CHRISTIAN

In *Gittin* (62a) it says:

"A Jew must not enter the home of a *Nokhri* on a feast day to offer him greetings. However, if he meets him on the street, he may offer him a greeting, but curtly and with head bowed."

2. A JEW MUST NOT RETURN THE GREETINGS OF A CHRISTIAN

In *Iore Dea* (148, 10) it says:

"A Jew must not return the greeting of a Christian by bowing before him.

It is good, therefore, to salute him first and so avoid having to answer him back if the *Akum* salutes him first."

Rabbi Kohana says that when a Jew salutes a Christian he should say "Peace to my Lord," but intend this for his own Rabbi. For the Tosephtoth says: "For his heart was turned towards his own Rabbi."

3. A JEW MUST NOT GO BEFORE A CHRISTIAN JUDGE

In *Choschen Hammischpat* (26,1) it says:

"A Jew is not permitted to bring his case before *Akum* judges, even if the matter is judged by the decisions of Jewish law, and even if both parties agree to abide by such decisions. He who does so is impious and similar to one who calumniates and blasphemes, and who raises his hand against the Law given us by Moses, our great law-giver. Hagah says 'The *Bethin* has the power to excommunicate such a one until he releases his Jewish brother from the hands of the Gentile.'"

4. A CHRISTIAN CANNOT BE USED AS A WITNESS

In *Choschen Ham.* (34, 19) it says:

"A *Goi* or a servant is not capable of acting as a witness."

5. A JEW CANNOT EAT CHRISTIAN FOOD

In *Iore Dea* (112, 1) it says: "The Elders forbade the eating of the bread of the *Akum,* lest we would seem to be familiar with them."

And in *Abhodah arah* (35b) it says:

"The following things belonging to the *Goim* are forbidden: Milk which a *Goi* takes from a cow, in the absence of a Jew; also their bread, etc."

6. A JEW MUST NEVER ACT IN ANY WAY LIKE A CHRISTIAN

In *Iore Dea* (178, 1) it says:

"It is not permitted to imitate the customs of the *Akum,* nor to act like them. Nor is it permitted to wear clothes like the *Akum,* not to comb the hair as they do...neither must Jews build houses that look like temples of the *Akum."*

Since, however, it is not possible to observe all these rules in every place, the *Hagah* says that they can be overlooked to a certain extent when, for instance, it is to the advantage of the Jew to do so; for example, if a Jew would profit by a trade which requires a certain kind of dress.

* * * * *

**Article II. - Christians Are to Be Avoided - Because They Are Unclean**

It is not known how often Jews must wash and purify themselves, nor how much they must study to avoid everything which might render them unclean. The Talmud teaches, however, that Christians are people whose touch alone makes things unclean. In *Abhodah Zarah* (72b) it says:

"A certain man was pouring wine from one jar into another by means of a tube, when a *Goi* came along and touched the tube with his hand. As a result all the wine (in both jars) had to be thrown away."

Every vessel, therefore, must be washed which comes into the possession of a Jew from a Christian, although it has never been in use. In *Iore Dea* (120, 1) it says:

"If a Jew buys a vessel for use at table from an *Akum,* whether it is made of metal, glass or lead, even if it is new, he must wash it in a *Mikvah* [a large basin], or in a cistern which holds forty quarts of water.

**Article III. - Christians Are to Be Avoided - Because They Are Idolaters**

1. Lest a Jew be the occasion of sin to the idolatrous Christians, according to the precept in *Levit.* XIX, 14: *"Do not put a stumbling-block before the blind* - he must avoid all contact with them on the days when they worship their gods. In *Abhodah Zarah* (2a) it says:

"For three days before their idolatrous festivals it is not permitted to buy or sell them anything. It is also forbidden to give or take any help from them, to change any money with them, to pay them back any debts or allow them to pay back debts."

In the *Abhodah Zarah,* 78c (the *Perusch* of Maimonides, *fol.* 8) it says:

"All the festivals of the followers of Jesus are forbidden, and we must conduct ourselves towards them as we would towards idolators. The first day of the week is their principal feast, and it is therefore forbidden to do any business whatsoever with those who believe in Jesus on their Sabbath. We must observe the same rules on their Sabbath as we do on the feastdays of idolators, as the Talmud teaches."

2. A JEW MUST NOT USE ANYTHING WHICH PERTAINS TO THE WORSHIP OF CHRISTIANS

In *Iore Dea* (139, 1) it says:

"It is forbidden to have anything to do with idols and everything that is used in their form of worship, whether they are made by the *Akum* or by Jews."

3. IT IS FORBIDDEN TO SELL TO CHRISTIANS ANYTHING CONNECTED WITH THEIR IDOLATROUS WORSHIP

The *Abhodah Zarah* (14b, *Toseph)* says:

"It is always forbidden to sell incense to an idolatrous priest, for it is evident that when he asks for it he wants it for no other purpose but to offer it before his idol. Anyone, therefore, who would sell it to him sins against the precept which forbids us to place a stumbling-block before the blind. It is also forbidden to sell candles to gentiles for their Feat of Candles. Candles however may be sold to them on other days. Neither is it permitted to sell a chalice to a gentile which a Jew has bought after a *Goi* has broken it and thrown it away. It may only be sold again to a gentile after it has been completely made over. For after it has been broken just once it can be used still to hold the wine which is offered in honor of their idol." Then follows the prohibition as to the selling of books to Christian priests, as we have seen above. Even the work of binding such books is forbidden to a Jew. *In Iore Dea* (139, 15) it says:

"It is forbidden to bind the books of the *Akum,* with the exception of law books. It may be done, however, if refusal to do so should cause enmity, but only after every effort has been made to refuse such work."

Likewise in *Iore Dea* (151, 1, *Hagah*):

"It is not permitted to sell water to an *Akum* if it is known that it will be made into Baptismal water."

Mention is also made of many other things which it is forbidden to sell to Christians, such as: cloth from which priestly vestments and banners may be made; paper and ink which may be used for writing books pertaining to their divine worship. It is forbidden to sell, or even to rent, houses to Christians which will be used by them as a place of worship.

Nowadays, however, Jews trade with Christians, especially on Christian feast days, and also sell them houses knowing full well that certain Sacraments will be administered therein, such as Baptism, Holy Communion and Extreme Unction. The Talmud can give no reason for this, and in the *Abhodah Zarah* (2a, *Toseph*) it says:

"It is difficult to say by what right Jews nowadays trade with the *Goim* on their (evil) feast days. For although many of them commit all kinds of licentious acts and perversions on their feast days in honor of saints which they do not look upon as gods, yet every week they celebrate the Day of the Nazarene [Sunday] which has always been forbidden to us."

Bartenora, however, in his commentary on *Abhodah Zarah* (I, 2, fol. 7b) it says:

"Since, while we are in captivity, we cannot live without trading with them, and we depend upon them for our food and we must fear them, it is only forbidden to trade with them on their feast days. Furthermore, it is permitted nowadays to trade with them on the actual day of their feasts, because the Rabbis are convinced that they do not worship their idols just because they trade with us. And what is forbidden in this book must be taken as applying directly to idolatry."

Rabbi Tam, however, contends that the *Mischnah* only forbids the selling of things to idolaters which will be used by them in the worship of idols, since they rejoice and worship their idols because they obtain the things necessary for that worship. He explains it thus (in *Abhodah Zarah,* 2a, *Toseph*):

"No one should wonder at this custom of ours. For, although we look upon them as idolaters, they can only offer up what they buy for money. Hence, our gain and their joy is not the reason for this prohibition, for they have enough money for these things, even if we did not trade with them."

4. THIS PROHIBITION DOES NOT APPLY TO ATHEISTS

In *Iore Dea* (148, 5) it says:

"It is only permitted to send a gift to an *Akum* on one of their feast days if it is known that he does not believe in idols and does not worship them."

Maimonides has the same in *Hilkhoth Akum* (IX, 2):

"It is also wrong to send a gift to a *Goi* on their feast days unless it is certain that he does not believe in the worship of Christian idols, and does not serve them."

**Article IV. -Christians Are to Be Avoided - Because They Are Evil**

There is nothing that Jews are more convinced of than the harm which Christians can do to the children of Israel. Because of this, the rulers of the Chosen People have always instructed them not to accept any help from Christians who will always resort to murder, and to other crimes, whenever they cannot otherwise obtain their evil ends. Thus a Jew must not employ a Christian as a nurse, or as a teacher for his children, or as a doctor, a barber or an obstetrician.

1. NOT AS A NURSE

In *Iore Dea* (81, 7, *Hagah*) it says:

"A child must not be nursed by a *Nokhri,* if an Israelite can be had; for the milk of the *Nokhrith* hardens the heart of a child and builds up an evil nature in him."

2. NOT AS A TEACHER

In *Iore Dea* (153, 1, *Hagah*) it says:

"A child must not be given to the *Akum* to learn manners, literature or the arts, for they will lead him to heresy."

3. NOT AS A DOCTOR

In *Iore Dea* (155, 1) it says:

"When a Jew is wounded in any way, even so gravely that he would have to violate the Sabbath in having a doctor, he must not employ the services of a Christian (*Akum*) doctor who is not known to everyone in the neighborhood; for we must guard against the spilling of blood. Even when it is not known if the patient will live or die, such a doctor must not be allowed to attend him. If, however, he is sure to die, then such a doctor may attend him, since an extra hour of life is not much to lose. If the *Akum*insists that a certain medicine is good, you may believe him, but be sure not to buy it from him.

There are some who say that this holds only when the *Akum* offer help free, and that it can be accepted every time it is paid for. But it can be taken for granted that they would not harm a Jew just for the sake of a matter of money."

In *Pesachim* (25a) it says:

"Rabbi Jochanan says: medical help can be accepted from all except idolaters, fornicators and murderers."

4. NOT AS A BARBER

In *Iore Dea* (156,1 ) it says:

"You must not be shaven by an *Akum* unless your Jewish friends are with you. There are some who say that it is not permitted to be shaved by an *Akum* even when others are present, unless you can see yourself in a mirror."

5. NOT AS AN OBSTETRICIAN

In *Abhodah Zarah* (26a) it says:

"Our Rabbis have passed it down for us, that a foreign woman must never be allowed to act as midwife at the birth of a child of Israel, because they are given to the shedding of blood. The Elders say, however, that a foreign woman may perform this task provided there are other Jewish women present, but never alone. Rabbi Meir, however, says that it is not allowed even others are present. For they often crush the soft head of the child with their hands and kill it; and they can do this without being noticed by those who are present."

# CHAPTER II

# CHRISTIANS MUST BE EXTERMINATED

The followers of "that man," whose name is taken by the Jews to mean "May his name and memory be blotted out," are not otherwise to be regarded than as people whom it would be good to get rid of. They are called Romans and tyrants who hold captive the children of Israel, and by their destruction the Jews would be freed from this Fourth Captivity. Every Jew is therefore bound to do all he can to destroy that impious kingdom of the Edomites (Rome) which rules the whole world. Since, however, it is not always and everywhere possible to effect this extermination of Christians, the Talmud orders that they should be attacked at least indirectly, namely: by injuring them in every possible way, and by thus lessening their power, help towards their ultimate destruction.

Wherever it is possible a Jew should kill Christians, and do so without mercy.

**Article I. - Harm must be done to Christians**

A Jew is commanded to harm Christians wherever he can, both indirectly by not helping them in any way, and also directly by wrecking their plans and projects; neither must he save a Christian who is in danger of death.

**I. Good must not be done to Christians**

In *Zohar* (1, 25b) it says:

"Those who do good to the *Akum* . . . will not rise from the dead." At times it is permitted to do good to Christians, but only in order to help Israel, namely, for the sake of peace and to hide hatred of them. Maimonides in *Hilkhoth Akum* (X, 6) says:

"Needy Gentiles may be helped as well as needy Jews, for the sake of peace..."In *Iore Dea* (148, 12 *Hagah*) it says:

"Therefore if you enter a town and find them celebrating a feast, you may pretend to rejoice with them in order to hide your hatred. Those, however, who care about the salvation of their souls should keep away from such celebrations. You should make it known that it is a hateful thing to rejoice with them, if you can do so without incurring enmity."

1. IT IS NOT PERMITTED TO PRAISE A CHRISTIAN

In *Abhodah Zarah* (20, a, *Toseph*) it says:

"Do not say anything in praise of them, lest it be said: How good that *Goi* is!"

In this way they explain the words of *Deuteronomy* (VII, 2) ... *and thou shalt show no mercy unto them [Goim],* as cited in the *Gemarah.* Rabbi S. Iarchi explains this Bible passage as follows:

"Do not pay them any compliments; for it is forbidden to say: how good that *Goi* is."

In *Iore Dea* (151, 14) it says:

"No one is allowed to praise them or to say how good an *Akum* is. How much less to praise what they do or to recount anything about them which would redound to their glory. If, however, while praising them you intend to give glory to God, namely, because he has created comely creatures, then it is allowed to do so."

2. A JEW NOT ALLOWED TO MENTION THE THINGS WHICH CHRISTIANS USE FOR THEIR IDOLATROUS WORSHIP

In *Hilkhoth Akum* (V, 12) it says:

"It is also forbidden to make mention of the *Akum;* for it is written (*Exodus* XXIII, 13):...*and make no mention of other gods."*

3. THEIR IDOLS MUST BE SPOKEN OF WITH CONTEMPT

In *Iore Dea* (146, 15) it says:

"Their idols must be destroyed, or called by contemptuous names." *Ibidem,* (147, 5):

"It is permitted to deride idols, and it is forbidden to say to a *Goi:* May your God help you, or I hope you will succeed."

Rabbi Bechai, explaining the text of *Deuteronomy* about hating idolatry, says:

"The Scripture taught us to hate idols and to call them by ignominious names. Thus, if the name of a church is *Bethgalia* - "house of magnificence," it should be called *Bethkaria* - an insignificant house, a pigs' house, a latrine. For this word, *karia,* denotes a low-down, slum place."

In numerous places ignominious names are given by the Jews to Christian things. It will not be out of place to list a few of these names which they give to things and persons which are held holy and dear by Christians, as follows:

JESUS is ignominiously called *Jeschu* - which means, *May his name and memory be blotted out*. His proper name in Hebrew is *Jeschua,* which means Salvation.

MARY, THE MOTHER OF JESUS, is called *Charia* - dung, excrement (German Dreck). In Hebrew her proper name is *Miriam.*

CHRISTIAN SAINTS, the word for which in Hebrew *Kedoschim,* are called *Kededchim* (*cinaedos*) - feminine men (Fairies). Women saints are called *Kedeschoth,* whores.

SUNDAY is called the day of calamity.

FEAST OF CHRISTMAS is called *Nital,* denoting extermination.

EASTER is not called by the proper name *Pesach* (Passover), but Ketsach, meaning a cutting down; or *Kesach,* a Gallows.

A CHRISTIAN CHURCH is not called *Beth Hattefillah,* House of Prayer, but *Beth Hattiflah,* a House of Vanity, a House of Evil.

THE GOSPEL BOOKS are called *Aavon Gilaion,* Books of Iniquity.

CHRISTIAN SACRIFICES are called Dung Offerings. In the Jerusalem Talmud (fol. 13b) the following occurs:

"He who sees them *mezabbelim* (excrementing - sacrificing) before their idol, let him say (*Exod.* XXII, 20): *He that sacrificeth unto an idol shall be utterly destroyed."*

Rabbi Iarchi (referring to *Num.* XXV, 3) teaches that the Gentiles actually honor their God by excrementing before him.

A CHRISTIAN GIRL who works for Jews on their sabbath is called a *Schaw-wesschicksel,* Sabbath Dirt.

4. A JEW IS NOT ALLOWED TO GIVE GIFTS TO CHRISTIANS

In *Hilkohoth Akum* (X, 5) it says:

"It is forbidden to give gifts to the *Goim.* But it is permitted to give them to a convert who lives among the Jews; for it is said: To the traveller who stops in your cities, give it to him to eat, or sell it to a Gentile, that is sell it, not give it."

In *Iore Dea* (151, 11) it says:

"It is forbidden to give free gifts to the *Akum* with whom a Jew may not treat familiarly."

The Talmud, however, allows a Jew to give gifts to Gentiles who are known to himand from whom he has hope of getting something in return.

5. A JEW IS FORBIDDEN TO SELL HIS FARM TO CHRISTIANS

In *Iore Dea* (334, 43) it says:

"In 24 cases a Jew must be repudiated, namely ...8. Anyone who sells his farm to the *Akum* must be sent into exile - unless he undertakes to make up for all the harm that follows as a consequence of having the *Akum* live near the Jews."

6. IT IS FORBIDDEN TO TEACH A TRADE TO CHRISTIANS

In *Iore Dea* (154, 2) it says:

"It is not permitted to teach any trade to the *Akum."*

**II. Harm must be done to the Work of Christians**

Since the *Goim* minister to Jews like beasts of burden, belong to a Jew together with his life and all his faculties:

"The life of a *Goi* and all his physical powers belong to a Jew." (A. Rohl. *Die Polem.* p.20)

It is an axiom of the Rabbis that a Jew may take anything that belongs to Christians for any reason whatsoever, even by fraud; nor can such be called robbery since it is merely taking what belongs to him.

In *Babba Bathra* (54 b) it says:

"All things pertaining to the *Goim* are like a desert; the first person to come along and take them can claim them for his own."

1. CHRISTIANS MUST NOT BE TOLD IF THEY PAY TOO MUCH TO A JEW

In *Choschen Hammischpat* (183, 7) it says:

"If you send a messenger to collect money from an *Akum* and the *Akum* pays too much, the messenger may keep the difference. But if the messenger does not know about it, then you may keep it all yourself."

2. LOST PROPERTY OF CHRISTIANS MUST NOT BE RETURNED TO THEM

In *Choschen Hamm.* (266, 1) it says:

"A Jew may keep anything he finds which belongs to the *Akum,* for it is written: *Return to thy brethren what is lost* (*Deuter.* XXII, 3). For he who returns lost property [to Christians] sins against the Law by increasing the power of the transgressors of the Law. It is praiseworthy, however, to return lost property if it is done to honor the name of God, namely, if by so doing Christians will praise the Jews and look upon them as honorable people."

3. CHRISTIANS MAY BE DEFRAUDED

In *Babba Kama* (113b) it says:

"It is permitted to deceive a *Goi."*

And in *Choschen Hamm.* (156, 5 *Hagah*) it says:

"If a Jew is doing good business with an *Akum* it is not allowed to other Jews, in certain places, to come and do business with the same *Akum. In other places,* however, it is different, where another Jews is allowed to go to the same *Akum,* lead him on, do business with him and to deceive him and take his money. For the wealth of the *Akum* is to be regarded as common property and belongs to the first who can get it. There are some, however, who say that this should not be done."

In *Choschen Hamm.* (183, 7 *Hagah*) it says:

"If a Jew is doing business with an *Akum* and a fellow Israelite comes along and defrauds the *Akum,* either by false measure, weight or number, he must divide his profit with his fellow Israelite, since both had a part in the deal, and also in order to help him along."

4. A JEW MAY PRETEND HE IS A CHRISTIAN TO DECEIVE CHRISTIANS

In *Iore Dea* (157, 2 *Hagah*) it says:

"If a Jew is able to deceive them [idolaters] by pretending he is a worshipper of the stars, he may do so."

5. A JEW IS ALLOWED TO PRACTICE USURY ON CHRISTIANS

In *Abhodah Zarah* (54a) it says:;

"It is allowed to take usury from Apostates who fall into idolatry."

And in *Iore Dea* (159, 1) it says:

"It is permitted, according to the *Torah,* to lend money to an *Akum* with usury. Some of the Elders, however, deny this except in a case of life and death. Nowadays it is permitted for any reason."

## III. Christians may be harmed in Legal Matters

1. A JEW MAY LIE AND PERJURE HIMSELF TO CONDEMN A CHRISTIAN

In *Babba Kama* (113a) it says:

"Our teaching is as follows: When a Jew and a *Goi* come into court, absolve the Jew, if you can, according to the laws of Israel. If the *Goi* wins, tell him that is what our laws require. If however, the Jew can be absolved according to the gentile law, absolve him and say it is due to our laws. If this cannot be done proceed callously against the *Goim,* as Rabbi Ischmael advises. Rabbi Akibha, however, holds that you cannot act fraudulently lest you profane the Name of God, and have a Jew commited for perjury."

A marginal note, however, explains this qualification of Rabbi Akibha as follows:

"The name of God is not profaned when it is not known by the *Goi* that the Jew has lied."

And further on, the *Babba Kama* (113b) says:

"The name of God is not profaned when, for example, a Jew lies to a *Goi* by saying: 'I gave something to your father, but he is dead; you must return it to me,' as long as the *Goi* does not know that you are lying."

2. A JEW MAY PERJURE HIMSELF WITH A CLEAR CONSCIENCE

In *Kallah* (1b, p.18) it says:

"She (the mother of the *mamzer*) said to him, 'Swear to me.' And Rabbi Akibha swore with his lips, but in his heart he invalidated his oath."

A similar text is found in *Schabbuoth Hagahoth* of Rabbi Ascher (6d):

"If the magistrate of a city compels Jews to swear that they will not escape from the city nor take anything out of it, they may swear falsely by saying to themselves that they will not escape today, nor take anything out of the city today only."

**IV. Christians must be harmed in Things Necessary for Life**

Jews must spare no means in fighting the tyrants who hold them in this Fourth Captivity in order to set themselves free. They must fight Christians with astuteness and do nothing to prevent evil from happening to them: their sick must not be cared for, Christian women in childbirth must not be helped, nor must they be saved when in danger of death.

1. A JEW MUST ALWAYS TRY TO DECEIVE CHRISTIANS

In *Zohar* (I, 160a) it says:

"Rabbi Jehuda said to him [Rabbi Chezkia]: 'He is to be praised who is able to free himself from the enemies of Israel, and the just are much to be praised who get free from them and fight against them. 'Rabbi Chezkia asked, 'How must we fight against them?' Rabbi Jehuda said, *'By wise counsel thou shalt war against them' (Proverbs,* ch. 24, 6). By what kind of war? The kind of war that every son of man must fight against his enemies, which Jacob used against Esau - by deceit and trickery whenever possible. They must be fought against without ceasing, until proper order be restored. Thus it is with satisfaction that I say we should free ourselves from them and rule over them."

2. A SICK CHRISTIAN MUST NOT BE AIDED

In *Iore Dea* (158, 1) it says:

"The *Akum* are not to be cured, even for money, unless it would incur their enmity."

3. A CHRISTIAN WOMAN IN CHILDBIRTH MUST NOT BE HELPED

In *Orach Chaiim* (330, 2) it says:

"No help is to be given to an *Akun* woman in labor on the sabbath, even in a small way, for the Sabbath must not be violated."

4. A CHRISTIAN IN DANGER OF DEATH MUST NOT BE HELPED

In *Choschen Hamm.* (425, 5) it says:

"If you see a heretic, who does not believe in the *Torah,* fall into a well in which there is a ladder, hurry at once and take it away and say to him 'I have to go and take my son down from a roof; I will bring the ladder back to you at once' or something else. The Kuthaei, however, who are not our enemies, who take care of the sheep of the Israelites, are not to be killed directly, but they must not be saved from death."

And in *Iore Dea* (158, 1) it says:

"The *Akum* who are not enemies of ours must not be killed directly, nevertheless they must not be saved from danger of death. For example, if you see one of them fall into the sea, do not pull him out unless he promises to give you money."

Maimonides, in *Hilkhoth Akum* (X, 1) says:

"Do not have pity for them, for it is said (*Deuter.* VII, 2): *Show no mercy unto them.* Therefore, if you see an *Akum* in difficulty or drowning, do not go to his help. And if he is in danger of death, do not save him from death. But it is not right to kill him by your own hand by shoving them into a well or in some other way, since they are not at war with us."

**Article II. - Christians are to be Killed**

Lastly, the Talmud commands that Christians are to be killed without mercy. In the *Abhodah Zarah* (26b) it says:

"Heretics, traitors and apostates are to be thrown into a well and not rescued."And in *Choschen Hammischpat* (388, 10) it says:

"A spy is to be killed, even in our days, wherever he is found. He may be killed even before he confesses. And even if he admits that he only intended to do harm to somebody, and if the harm which he intended is not very great, it is sufficient to have him condemned to death. He must be warned, however, not to confess to this. But if he impudently says 'No, I will confess it!' then he must be killed, and the sooner the better.

If there is no time to warn him, it is not necessary to do so. There are some who say that a traitor is to be put to death only when it is impossible to get rid of him by mutilating him, that is, by cutting out his tongue or his eyes, but if this can be done he must not be killed, since he is not any worse than others who persecute us."

And in *Choschen Hamm.* again (388, 15) it says:

"If it can be proved that someone has betrayed Israel three times, or has given the money of Israelites to the *Akum,* a way must be found after prudent consideration to wipe him off the face of the earth."

### I. Renegades to be Killed

Even a Christian who is found studying the Law of Israel merits death. In *Sanhedrin* (59a) it says:

"Rabbi Jochanan says: A *Goi* who pries into the Law is guilty to death."

### II. Baptized Jews are to be Put to Death

In *Hilkhoth Akum* (X, 2) it says:

"These things [supra] are intended for idolaters. But Israelites also, who lapse from their religion and become epicureans, are to be killed, and we must persecute them to the end. For they afflict Israel and turn the people from God."

And in *Iore Dea* (158, 2 *Hagah*) it says:

"Renegades who turn to the pleasures of the *Akum,* and who become contaminated with them by worshipping stars and planets as they do, are to be killed."

Likewise in *Choschen Hamm.* (425, 5) it says:

"Jews who become epicureans, who take to the worship of stars and planets and sin maliciously; also those who eat the flesh of wounded animals, or who dress in vain clothes, deserve the name of epicureans; likewise those who deny the Torah and the Prophets of Israel - the law is that all those should be killed; and those who have the power of life and death should have them killed; and if this cannot be done, they should be led to their death by deceptive methods."

Rabbi Maimonides, in *Hilkhoth Teschubhah* (III, 8) gives the list of those who are considered as denying the Law:

"There are three classes of people who deny the Law of the Torah: (1) Those who say that the Torah was not given by God, at least one verse or one word of it, and who say that it was all the work of Moses; (2) Those who reject the explanation of the Torah, namely, the Oral Law of the *Mischnah,* and do not recognize the authority of the Doctors of the Law, like the followers of *Tsadok* (Sadducees) and *Baithos;* (3) Those who say that God changed the Law for another New Law, and that the Torah no longer has any value, although they do not deny that it was given by God, as the Christians and the Turks believe. All of these deny the Law of the Torah."

**III. Christians are to be Killed because They are Tyrants**

In *Zohar* (I, 25a) it says:

"The People of the Earth are idolaters, and it has been written about them: *Let them be wiped off the face of the earth. Destroy the memory of the Amalekites.* They are with us still in this Fourth Captivity, namely, the Princes [of Rome]...who are really Amalakites."

1. THESE PRINCES ARE TO BE KILLED FIRST

For if they are allowed to live, the hope of the liberation of the Jews is in vain, and their prayers for release from this Fourth Captivity are of no avail. In *Zohar* (I, 219B) it says:

"It is certain that our captivity will last until the princes of the gentiles who worship idols are destroyed."

And again in *Zohar* (II, 19a) it says:

"Rabbi Jehuda said: Come and see how it is; how the princes have assumed power over Israel and the Israelites make no outcry. But their rejoicing is heard when the prince falls. It is written that: the King of the Egyptians died and soon the children of Israel were released from captivity; they cried out and their voice ascended to God."

2. THE PRINCEDOM WHOSE CHIEF CITY IS ROME IS THE ONE TO BE HATED MOST OF ALL BY THE JEWS

They call it the Kingdom of Esau, and of the Edomites, the Kingdom of Pride, the Wicked Kingdom, Impious Rome. The Turkish Empire is called the Kingdom of the Ismaelites which they do not wish to destroy. The Kingdom of Rome, however, must be exterminated, because when corrupt Rome is destroyed, salvation and freedom will come to God's Chosen People.

Rabbi David Kimchi writes as follows in *Obadiam:*

"What the Prophets foretold about the destruction of Edom in the last days was intended for Rome, as Isaiah explains (ch. 34, 1): *Come near, ye nations, to hear* . . . For when Rome is destroyed, Israel shall be redeemed."

Rabbi Abraham also, in his book *Tseror Hammor,* section *Schoftim,* says the same:

"Immediately after Rome is destroyed we shall be redeemed."

**IV. Lastly, all Christians, including the Best of Them, are to be Killed**

In *Abhodah Zarah* (26b, *Tosephoth*) it says:

"Even the best of the *Goim* should be killed"

The Schulchan Arukh, after the words of *Iore Dea* (158, 1) that those of the *Akum* who do no harm to Jews are not to be killed, namely those who do not wage war against Israel, thus explains the word *Milchamah* - war:

"But in time of war the *Akum* are to be killed, for it is written: 'The good among the Akum deserve to be killed, etc.'"

**V. A Jew who Kills a Christian Commits No Sin, but Offers an Acceptable Sacrifice to God**

In *Speher Or Israel* (177b) it says:

"Take the life of the Kliphoth and kill them, and you will please God the same as one who offers incense to Him."

And in *Ialkut Simoni* (245c. n. 772) it says:

"Everyone who sheds the blood of the impious is as acceptable to God as he who offers a sacrifice to God."

**VI. After the Destruction of the Temple at Jerusalem, the only Sacrifice Nexessary is the Extermination of Christians**

In *Zohar* (III, 227b) the *Good Pastor* says:

"The only sacrifice required is that we remove the unclean from amongst us."

*Zhoar* (II, 43a), explaining the precept of Moses about the redemption of the first born of an ass by offering a lamb, says:

"The ass means the non-Jew, who is to be redeemed by the offering of a lamb, which is the dispersed sheep of Israel. But if he refuses to be redeemed, then break his skull....They should be taken out of the book of the living, for it is said about them: He who sins against me, I shall take out of the book of life."

**VII. Those Who Kill Christians shall have a High Place in Heaven**

In *Zohar* (I, 28b, and 39a) it says:

"In the palaces of the fourth heaven are those who lamented over Sion and Jerusalem, and all those who destroyed idolatrous nations...and those who killed off people who worship idols are clothed in purple garments so that they may be recognized and honored."

**VIII. Jews must Never Cease to Exterminate the Goim; They must Never Leave them in Peace and Never Submit to Them**

In *Hilhoth Akum* (X, 1)it says:

"Do not eat with idolaters, nor permit them to worship their idols; for it is written: *Make no covenant with them, nor show mercy unto them (Deuter.* ch. 7, 2). Either turn away from their idols or kill them."

*Ibidem* (X, 7):

"In places where Jews are strong, no idolater must be allowed to remain..."

**IX. All Jews are Obliged to Unite Together to Destroy Traitors among Them**

In *Choschen Hamm.* (338, 16) it says:

"All the inhabitants of a city are obliged to contribute to the expense of killing a traitor, even those who have to pay other taxes."

**X.No Festival, no matter how solemn, must Prevent the Beheading of a Christian**

In *Pesachim* (49b) it says:

"Rabbi Eliezer said: It is permitted to cut off the head of an 'idiot' [one of the people of the Earth] on the feast of the Atonement when it falls on the Sabbath. His disciples said to him: Rabbi, you should rather say *to sacrifice.* But he replied: By no means, for it is necessary to pray while sacrificing, and there is no need of prayers when you behead someone."

**XI. The One Object of all the Actions and Prayers of the Jews should be to Destroy the Christian Religion**

Thus the Jews picture their Messiah and Liberator whom they expect, as a persecutor who will inflict great calamities upon non-Jews. The Talmud lists three great evils which will come upon the world when the Messiah comes. In *Schabbath* (118a) it says:

"Whoever eats three meals on the Sabbath shall be saved from the three evils: from the punishments of the Messiah, from the pain of hell and from the war of Magog; for it is written: *Behold, I shall send you Elias the Prophet before the coming of the 'Day' of the Lord, etc.**

**XII. In their Prayers the Jews sigh for the Coming of the Revengeful Messiah, especially on the Eve of the Passover:**

*"pour out thy anger upon nations that know thee not, and upon the kingdoms which do not invoke thy name; Pour out thy indignation upon them, and let thy wrathful anger take hold of them; Persecute and destroy them in anger from under the heavens of the Lord."*

They also pray as follows:

*"How long will thy strength remain captive and thy beauty lie under the hand of the oppressor? O God! Show forth thy strength and thy zeal against our enemies; break their strength and let them be confounded..."*

And again:

*"Cut off the hope of the unjust; let all heretics perish at once; root out, break up and destroy the Proud Kingdom; hasten to make all peoples subject in our days."*

* * *

At that very same time, on Good Friday, that "Prince of the Proud Empire" of Rome, the Pope, prays, and orders everyone in the world to pray for all "heretics" and those who are "lost", as follows:

*"Let us pray for the perfidious Jews: that the Lord our God may take away the veil from their hearts, that they may acknowledge Jesus Christ our Lord.*

*"Omnipotent and Eternal God, who does not even exclude Jewish perfidy from thy mercy: hear our prayers which we offer for the blindness of that people, that, having recognized the light of thy truth, which is Christ, they may come out of their darkness, Through Jesus Christ our Lordà..."*